Personalisation

Practical thoughts and ideas from
people making it happen

Edited by Sam Newman

OLM-Pavilion

Contents

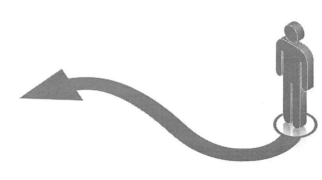

Foreword

Personalisation is a word that was hardly used in a social care context – or in any other for that matter – until only a few years ago. Now, not just a buzzword, but a term that has come to signify and represent probably the biggest change in social work and social care practice for a generation.

It didn't come from nowhere, of course. It has a deep history in the social work profession and stems very much from those debates in the 80s and 90s, which were focused on an altogether different concept – 'empowerment'. The arguments then were largely progressed via the old Central Council for the Education and Training of Social Workers and the National Institute for Social Work, the immediate precursors of our current GSCC and SCIE.

They centred on asking how the most liberal of all professions could work with those who it then called 'clients' in a way that truly liberated them – not just from the oppressive nature of the silo-like structures that social services by then had largely become, but also from the very nature of the professional–client relationship.

At the time social workers beat their breasts about how to improve practice in conducting that relationship with their clients in a less oppressive way. But it wasn't just the cynics who thought that the underlying power relationship between client and professional could not be altered until some adjustment was made in the control of the services available, and the money used to purchase them.

The breakthrough came – largely pioneered by the former ADSS – with the development of direct payments, putting financial responsibility into the hands of users and through that, firmly rebalancing the power relationship in hard, financial terms.

Originally the passion of physically disabled people and their carers, the ideas fast spread to people with mental health problems, learning disabilities, their carers and eventually to older people as well. Few thought that the debates of the mid-90s would lead to the full-blown social policy revolution that it has become. But the phenomenon of personalisation, as it extends from those early beginnings into the broad social care economy and indeed beyond, is their direct successor.

This handbook documents its successes and tribulations. It shows us 'how' and moves us on from the 'whether'. It shows personalisation operating across the board. It will prove an important tool for all those authorities, which as we begin to move into year two of the transformation agenda, are beginning to reach some crunch decisions about the way ahead.

As well as showing us the future, it also provides an important database for people on the front line to contact people who've already been there. It is an invaluable tool for leading everyone involved to a place where they can discuss emerging issues with those colleagues, then tailor their own local solutions with the benefit of the advice that's available, and which has been so successfully documented in this publication.

John Dixon,
immediate past president, Association of Directors of Adult Social Services

Personalisation: Practical thoughts and ideas from people making it happen   © OLM-Pavilion 2009

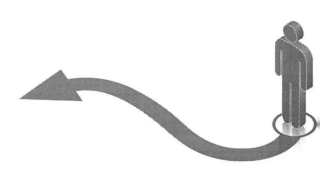

Contributors

David Abbey, MySafeHome's director, has worked in the financial services sector since 1984 and is a fully qualified financial adviser. Back in 1997 he was invited to join a 'steering group' to develop a process that would enable people with a disability to buy a home of their own. At the time, the challenges that this presented seemed insurmountable, however, thanks to the support of key figures in the disability sector, housing associations, social workers, an open-minded lender and the drive of parents, carers and the potential buyers themselves, a unique shared ownership model was developed and launched. David then established MySafeHome to provide all of the help and support that everyone involved in helping disabled buyers to realise their dream of home ownership needs. Passionate about the personalisation agenda, David is a regular speaker at major disability events and the UK's acknowledged expert in home ownership for people with a disability.

Lord Victor Adebowale is chief executive of Turning Point, the UK's leading social care organisation, which has more than 200 services nationwide. Turning Point works with people facing a range of complex needs including substance misuse, mental health problems and learning disabilities. Victor began his career in local authority estate management before joining the housing association movement. He spent time with Patchwork Community Housing Association, was director of the Alcohol Recovery Project and was most recently the chief executive of the leading youth homelessness charity Centrepoint. Victor is involved in a number of taskforce groups, advising the government on mental health, substance misuse, learning disability and the role of the voluntary sector. He is co-chair of the Ministerial Advisory Group on Mental Health, a member of the Advisory Council on the Misuse of Drugs and an audit commissioner. In 2000 Victor was awarded a CBE in the New Year's Honours List for services to the New Deal, the unemployed and homeless young people. A year later, Victor became one of the first people to be appointed as a people's peer and in 2007 he became one of the government's social enterprise ambassadors.

Geoff Baines originally trained as a social worker and has been working with people with learning disabilities and their families for the last 24 years. His work has included individual support, operational management of both specialist health and social care

services, commissioning, and senior management of integrated health and social care services. Geoff was the director of the change team that assisted the Cornwall community in developing and implementing changes recommended by a joint investigation into services provided by the Cornwall Partnership NHS Trust for people with learning disabilities. This work led to the successful lifting of special measures in March 2008. Geoff is currently an associate director for the NHS South West Strategic Health Authority with a lead role in learning disability, mental health and children's services. He is actively involved on a multi-agency basis with local and regional organisations, and also represents strategic health authorities at a national level, assisting in the roll-out of national policy.

Tony Bennett has worked for the Department of Health, social services and various small support organisations. Tony is a qualified teacher and citizen leader who has held various retail management positions. He spent time with the fledgling Business Link organisation at its inception, attending training delivered by Durham University Business School. Following this, he spent several years in general management in smaller companies in Lincolnshire. Tony cared full-time for his father who had Alzheimer's disease and secured him an individual budget in the Lincolnshire individual budget pilot scheme. Tony is currently self-employed and runs Carben Consultancy and Training, which specialises in personalisation and transforming adult social care. He is a passionate advocate of self-directed support.

Rosemary Berks is with Darlington Association on Disability.

Lorna Campbell is a local councillor in Lambeth and a cabinet member for health and well-being. Her portfolio covers older people, disabilities, mental health issues, people with or affected by HIV or Aids, carers, Careline, sheltered housing support, adult residential care, and working with the voluntary sector and faith groups. Prior to her current role, Lorna was a deputy cabinet member for community cohesion, during which time she chaired the executive commission on guns, gangs and violent crime. Lorna is a member of the Black Asian and Minority Ethnic (BAME) Women Councillors' Taskforce and was also involved in the development of the Black Londoners Forum, serving on the executive for two years, as well as on the council of the London Civic Forum. Lorna's professional background is in communications and customer services. She has a BA (Hons) in law and politics and a PGDip in black theology.

Joolz Casey was a member of the team that created the model of self-directed support and for over four years has led work on the workforce agenda. A qualified learning disability nurse, Joolz spent over 10 years moving people into community services before becoming the head of learning and development for Mencap.

Mel Cassedy is the strategic business manager for adult and community services in Suffolk County Council and has been working for the Council for 40 years come October. Mel started his career as a trainee accountant and became a fully qualified Chartered Institute of Public Finance and Accountancy member in 1975, later progressing through a variety of professional roles in corporate finance. In 1988, he secured a secondment as head of finance in Suffolk social services, eventually becoming an assistant director of resources in 1992. In the mid-1990s he led on the introduction of Care First in Suffolk. In 2004, with the split of social services into adult and children's services, Mel gave up his finance role and since then has had responsibility for commissioning, performance management, quality assurance, the supporting people programme, workforce development, adult and community learning, business support, a client-led role for human resources and IT developments.

Jo Cleary is executive director of adults' and community services, London Borough of Lambeth.

Terry Dafter is director of adult social care, Stockport Metropolitan Borough Council.

Nick Dixon is a qualified social worker who practised in childcare for seven years, as well as working as an approved social worker for around nine years. He was a team manager and service manager within mental health services between 1997 and 2002. In 2008, following working for Pennine Care Mental Health Trust for five years as the head of social care in Stockport, Nick moved into a commissioning role initially on behalf of Stockport Metropolitan Borough Council, and in the last year as a joint commissioning manager working across the council and the primary care trust. His current role is to support the implementation of the Stockport Mental Health Joint Commissioning Strategy (2007–2012), taking a lead on key social care priorities such as implementing the recovery approach, the mental health social inclusion strategy, meaningful user and carer involvement and self-directed support.

Peter Hay is director of adult social care, Birmingham City Council

Jo Hogg is a freelance consultant based in North Somerset. Jo has supported people with learning disabilities and their families for more than 20 years, working in supported living, day services and supported employment. She spent six years working for KeyRing – Living Support Networks and developed the first KeyRing networks outside London. She has been working with individuals, families and local authorities to develop individualised housing and support options. She has worked for housing and support partnerships, the Valuing People support team and Partners for Inclusion (East Renfrewshire). In April 2006 Jo joined the Cornwall Change Team and supported the closure of Budock, Tamarisk and West Heath hospitals and the development of more

personalised services. Jo is presently working with organisations and local authorities in England and Scotland, developing personalised alternatives to traditional models of housing and support, including the re-provision of NHS campus services.

Jeff Jerome began working as national director for Social Care Transformation in October 2008, having been the director of adult and community services at the London Borough of Richmond for the previous seven years. His current role, working across local government to develop the personalisation agenda for social care, is government funded and accountable to a consortium of the Improvement and Development Agency for local government (IDeA), the Local Government Association, the Association of Directors of Adult Social Services (ADASS) and the Department of Health. Jeff began his career in the NHS working with stroke patients and has worked in local government for 34 years in the field of social services and housing. This has included roles at Manchester City Council and six London boroughs. In the late 1990s, Jeff's personal experience in managing direct payments on behalf of his sister instilled in him a belief in the importance of personalising public care services. His subsequent interest in the care of people with long-term and progressive conditions led to him chairing the ADASS Disabilities Network and getting involved in a number of key national initiatives.

Doreen Kelly has worked with people with mental health and learning disabilities since 1982. After qualifying as a nurse, she moved to the not-for-profit sector to work with people leaving institutional settings. Doreen is now the director of Partners for Inclusion, which she set-up nine years ago to provide tailor-made support for people with learning and mental health disabilities. The organisation is committed to person-centred values and focuses on making the most of community support and the relationships in an individual's life. Following an investigation into services provided by the Cornwall Partnership NHS Trust, Doreen was one of the consultants involved in helping people to leave Buddock hospital. As well as this, Doreen has worked with Professor Mansell and the Valuing People Support Team to roll out recommendations made in the recent Mansell report. Doreen is also a board member of In Control Scotland and a founding member of Neighbourhood Networks – a Scottish organisation based on the KeyRing model.

Lynn Laws is a founding director of SCP Consult, established five years ago, and is the company lead on safeguarding adults. Lynn is an experienced consultant in both operational and strategic development of health and social care services, with extensive knowledge across all service groups. As a freelance consultant, Lynn has a proven track record at senior management level, and has led a range of complex service improvement projects for a number of local authorities.

Sian Lockwood is a qualified social worker who worked in a range of statutory and voluntary sector organisations in the UK and Africa before becoming, in 1991, the chief executive of a charity in the north of England, which provided a variety of community and family-based services including Shared Lives (adult placement). Sian was elected chair of NAAPS UK (the umbrella organisation representing Shared Lives and other small community services in the UK) in 2002 and in that role worked closely with the UK government to promote the value of small, localised services and ensure that legislative and regulatory requirements were appropriate and did not place unnecessary barriers in the way of people establishing and delivering good micro services. She has been able to continue and extend this work since her appointment as the charity's first chief executive in July 2004.

Alex MacNeil worked as part of the In Control team for the last two years, leading on events and working on people and provider development. Having worked in social care since 1992, Alex has managed and developed residential and supported living services before becoming Mencap's project manager for new learning.

Andrew McCulloch has been chief executive of the Mental Health Foundation for six years. Prior to his appointment, Andrew was director of policy at The Sainsbury Centre for Mental Health for six years, where he established a reputation as a leading authority on mental health policy. He was formerly a senior civil servant in the Department of Health for 16 years and was responsible for mental health and learning disabilities policy from 1992 to 1996. He has spoken and published widely on mental health issues. Andrew's other experience has included being a school governor, the non-executive director of an NHS trust, and the chair of mental health media. He has chaired or served on a range of national advisory committees and is mental health adviser to the National Endowment for Science, Technology and the Arts. He has a PhD in psychology from the University of Southampton and has a special interest in lifespan developmental psychology and adjustment to later life.

Sam Newman is director of OLM's personalisation programme, which is supporting councils to implement personalisation, and share best practice. Sam recently led, with David Todd of Symmetric and Tony Bennett, the ADASS sponsored Common RAS Programme working with 18 councils and eight citizen leaders. Prior to his current role Sam held several posts within the health and social care system, most recently as assistant director for adult social care in Devon County Council. Sam is a professionally qualified social worker.

Steven Rose began his career working with people with learning disabilities in 1974 in the NHS. Steven has been the chief executive of Choice Support since 1991. He has steered its growth and development from an organisation with a £1 million

turnover and just 11 employees, to one with a current turnover approaching £40 million and employing over 1,500 staff, providing services to around 750 people with learning disabilities. Choice Support enjoys a well-deserved reputation as being a leading provider of services for people with learning disabilities and is currently at the forefront of developing highly individualised services in response to the government's personalisation agenda. Steven retains an active interest in the health of people with learning disabilities and recently completed five years' service as a non-executive director of a primary care trust. He is a founding director of the Association for Supported Living and the editor of *Community Connecting*.

Helen Sanderson leads HSA, a development, training and consultancy team focused on person-centred approaches, support planning and review. Helen also designs and facilitates events for the Department of Health and local organisations.

Belinda Schwehr practised as a barrister in the mid-1980s before she took a specialist Master's degree in public law in 1990. Belinda then taught public law in university law schools but returned to professional practice in 1997, upon joining the Public Law Group at Rowe and Maw. She requalified as a solicitor in 1998, developing a specialist practice in adult social services, health care law and human rights. Her experience as a public speaker dates from this period when she began to offer training courses as a complementary adjunct to her litigation practice. Belinda now runs the legal website www.careandhealthlaw.com and is accredited by the Law Society to offer continuing professional development points to those attending her courses. She offers independent training and legal consultancy about the legal framework underpinning social care, and regularly appears at national conferences in England and Wales. In the last year she has been to over 50 health and care bodies to provide topical updates regarding the full range of policy, practice and performance issues. She has also advised the LGO, the HSC, the ADASS, NAFAO, charitable and private sector care home providers, domiciliary care and support providers, PCTs, users and carers.

Viv Slater is an independent consultant working with a number of local authorities to support their implementation of personalisation. She was formerly a member of the In Control team. Prior to that she was a key player in the 'engine room' of Oldham adult services in their pioneering approach to the implementation of personalisation – before it became policy and mainstream practice. This chapter is rooted in Viv's real experience of changing culture, challenging current risk aversion and ensuring that people really get to choose their support and their lives.

Sam Sly trained as a social worker and has worked in health, social care and regulation over the past 22 years. This has mainly been with people with learning disabilities or mental health needs. While working with CSCI (now CQC) Sam was

heavily involved in developing their user involvement strategies and has continued to give input to policy development since leaving the Commission. Sam was a member of the Change Team in Cornwall and facilitated the transfer of support services from Cornwall Partnership NHS Trust, as well as working on improving the quality of housing and support provided before and after transfer. Sam is currently managing one of the country's last NHS campus closure projects in Bournemouth, as well as continuing to promote the quality improvement of services being delivered to people with learning disabilities, through giving presentations about her experiences and personalisation, and training people to use a toolkit she developed while in Cornwall called Hands Off It's My Home – A path to Citizenship, which is now used nationally.

Jane Smith has been director of social services and housing in north Somerset since 2002 and director of adult social services and housing in 2005. She worked in the voluntary sector and trained and worked as a social worker in Liverpool before moving to the south west.

David Todd is a director of Symmetric SD Ltd. Symmetric is a small company that specialises in supporting public sector organisations in their change efforts. Symmetric utilises a strong systems thinking and system dynamics method and process to support all its work and uses these methods to embrace complexity and, in the process, develop a holistic understanding of the systems we operate within and create actions that are meaningful and sustainable. David has over 10 years experience in public sector projects across a wide range of areas including learning disabilities financial modelling, design and implementation of personalisation programmes for a number of local authorities, strategic review and redesign of NHS and social care services, detailed demand and capacity modelling within primary care mental health, and the redesign of services for children and their families. He is also a founding partner of Synergia, a New Zealand based consultancy that specialises in complex policy development and change projects in the public sector. He has a Master's degree in commerce (operations management) from Auckland University.

The User and Carer Forum, Scotland (formerly Panel) is a diverse group of people who have demonstrated leadership in their own lives and collectively by developing principles and standards of citizen leadership. They have built on the work of the User and Carer Panel, which was set up to ensure that people with experience of using social work services and carers had an influence on the 21st century review of social work services in Scotland, Changing Lives. Authors of the chapter are Debbie Berry, Sam Cairns, Andrew Denovan, Pru Davies, John Dow, George Johnstone, Jane Hope, Monica Hunter, Rana Mohammad Azam Khan, Lilian Lawson, Billi Love, Thomas McDougall, James McKillop, Isabel Moore and Jim Wagstaff, with support from Lisa Curtice, Laura Finnan Cowan, Andy Miller and Ruth Murphy at the Scottish Consortium for Learning Disability (SCLD).

John Wallace obtained a first class honours degree in electrical/electronic engineering from Leeds University in 1969 and a Master of Philosophy degree in 1970 for research into switched electronic filters. He spent three years at British Aerospace as a systems engineer working on communications satellites before joining the CEGB in 1973. At privatisation of the electricity supply industry he joined Nuclear Electric as an engineering project manager before retiring in 1995. He has a disabled son with a complex mixture of physical and mental health difficulties who now lives independently with support. His son has a direct payment for his care, but John provides his support through a contract with the local authority Supporting People team. John is a member of Inclusion South West (ISW), a registered community interest group that actively seeks to improve the quality of life of disabled people. Membership includes a number of family carers who manage and organise services for their relatives using direct payments, individuals who are themselves disabled and also some professionals working in health and social care. The group has particular expertise in person-centred planning and provides training for a wide range of professionals, family members and disabled individuals. It has a close relationship with the Valuing People team in the southwest and several members belong to local partnership boards and links. ISW members have been concerned about the empirical approach to resource allocation system development and John has recently deployed his professional engineering expertise to identify a more systematic approach.

Sarah Ward is the self-directed funding manager, adult and community services department, Hartlepool Borough Council.

Dawn Warwick is the director of adult social services in Wandsworth and co-chair of the Association of Directors of Adult Social Services (ADASS) Older People's Network. Dawn is also a trustee of ADASS. She has worked in social care for 26 years, starting her career as a social worker in Leicestershire. She later moved south to take the lead on mental health services in Hounslow. Dawn has held a number of senior management roles spanning children's and adult social care and prior to taking up her role in Wandsworth, was the deputy chief executive and strategic director for community and cultural services in Slough, where she was previously the director of social services from 2001.

Sarah Wood has previously been published under the writing name Anna Jacob. Sarah's experience as a parent carer has led to her becoming a person-centred planning facilitator, a partner in policy making, a citizen leader and more recently, becoming employed as a family carer expert with Self Direct. She is also part of the team developing the common resource allocation system and part of Lives Unlimited, a group that works towards creating support circles for local residents with disabilities and their families. Sarah is passionate about inclusion and self-directed support.

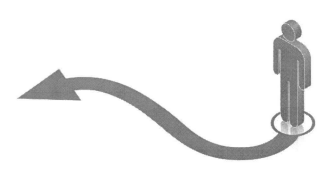

Introduction

Sam Newman

Not many years ago personalisation in social care and all that it stands for was just a twinkle in the eyes of a small number of people. They were called extremists, radicals, malcontents. They were accused of all sorts of bad behaviour usually reserved for people who are seen to be challenging the status quo.

Now personalisation is mainstream. It is supported by policy, and underpinned by a huge investment of public money to ensure it happens. Committed and enthusiastic people up and down the country are working out how to appropriately transfer power and control to people who need support to get on with their lives.

This is underpinned by the belief and the growing body of evidence that not only is this a more beneficial way of operating the social care system for the people who depend on it, but it is also a more effective way of investing scarce resources – creating better returns on investment. Measuring well-being and autonomy now become much more important than counting intensive packages of home care, or occupancy rates and unit costs of day centres and residential homes.

At the heart of this revolution is a radical reshaping of the perceptions of those people who need support – disabled people, older people, people with addictions – and all the familiar boxes we have put people into. The revolution requires us to readjust our perceptions and regard people not as clients or users – but as people who have a right to expect the same as everyone else – a reasonable place to live, enough money to lead a decent life, a network of loving and involved relationships that we all depend on for our continued well-being – and many more things besides. Personally speaking, my commitment to this transformation is underpinned by a deep misgiving about the ability of the conventional social care system to deliver these things in a respectful way, paying attention to people's human rights, rights to make mistakes, live life to the full, and self-determine how life will be.

This volume sets out to share and communicate just a few experiences of making this change happen – from a wide variety of people and organisations. Importantly there are a number of contributions from people themselves and their families – who must play a central role in changing the current system. Co-production and citizen leadership can be tokenistic words, but it is essential that social care works out a new relationship with the people and their families who need support. They are key players in creating a new system that really works for them. One of the symptoms of our current broken system is the institutionalised oppositional relationships that too often characterise the contact between family members and managers and staff within the system. I have seen at close quarters the negative and destructive outcomes of this dynamic for all people caught in its trap. Who can win in a system that encourages families and social workers to go and find the best service they can for someone, and then return to base to be told that the chosen service is unaffordable? It is just one compelling reason for radically changing the system that has caused those relationships to ensue – where families describe how they have had to 'fight' for decades to get a reasonable response for their loved ones, and good hearted committed social care people get caught in the crossfire from justifiably angry and tired families frustrated by yet another failure of the system to deliver the goods. Understanding the legal framework within which a new social care system operates, and making those legal issues transparent is just one important way in which people and families can exercise their rights and know what they are entitled to.

Housing issues appear early in this volume too. For most of us, where we live and who we live with are key decisions that we expect to have autonomy over, and without it, any system of support will fail. This contribution debunks myths that mainstream housing options can't work for people who need support (and I mean real mainstream housing options – involving estate agents, home information packs, conveyancing solicitors, leaky boilers etc.), are unaffordable, or are just a Rolls Royce solution for the few. As with many issues related to social care, the system needs to stop expecting itself to provide specialised solutions (in the form of institutional living or other specialised solutions) and cast itself as the catalyst that must create mainstream access that has been denied to some people in our community.

How we treat the money is also a key concept that we need to understand. The current system is supported by a particular attitude to social care finance that includes a mistaken belief that if we pre-purchase wholesale via highly bureaucratic tendering and contracting processes we will create value and efficiency. There is also an underlying myth at play in the current system that suggests that most if not all applicants are out to defraud it. It is vital that the money is individualised by whatever resource allocation system will work – not through a scientifically accurate process to the last penny, but as an assurance that people themselves can take control in whatever way

works for them, of how the money is invested. This calls into question the continuing role of 'commissioning' when we don't have control of the money anymore because people do, and I am grateful for the example contained here that describes how social care commissioning responsibilities can be redrawn – away from knowing best and spending money on people's behalf, to creating a system and an environment where people in control of their resources can make the choices that make sense to them.

Workforce issues are crucial – we can sort out the money but unless there are key shifts in attitudes and relationships not much will change. Having talked with hundreds of workers around the country both in and out of local authorities I am confident that the values and principles of personalisation are close to the hearts of most if not all. However, it is vital that we construct a new workforce framework that doesn't automatically inherit the old expectations in relation to skills, training, capacity and resources. I will always remember a conversation with a team leader of a support service who were committed to changing radically how they offered support. That team had to go through an experience that they described as 'unlearning' – letting go of their hard won assumptions about the people they were supporting, what the nature of their job is, and what skills and competencies they needed to offer. Whatever else we need, we need a large available personalised support workforce – both formal and informal – with no agenda, ready to listen and respond to the support needs of disabled people in a respectful and flexible way. So what does 'no agenda' mean?

One wise woman explained to me once how this might be. The system and people in it can bring to people who need support many gifts: expertise, experience, intelligence, knowledge, ideas about what is possible and what will enhance people's lives. These things can be a rich source of help. However we, the system, need, while doing this, to let go of our 'agenda' – whether it is political, professional, or otherwise. This is a liberating way to be, which enables us to meet people with real openness and humility, so we listen without 'inner noise' getting in the way. It is about having nothing to prove, and no expectations.

Having no agenda is not the same as having no purpose or intention. Our intention is likely to be something like: 'creating a relationship where the other person can make the best possible choices for themselves'. Having no agenda frees us to be fully present, open to the life and ideas of the person we are meeting, and to be more wholly ourselves.

As we listen deeply to the other, it is as if the attention we are offering to them makes us more able to 'hear' our own deeper thoughts as well. They are often thoughts we cannot get to by a structured logical pathway. It is important to check these thoughts: they are not infallible, but they can be a powerful source of insight.

There is no need to know better, or tell, or demonstrate our wisdom. In fact, having no agenda may turn out to be our most powerful source of wisdom.

So we need a system, and a workforce, that listens with no agenda – just waiting – to respond in the right way to enable people who need support to get the lives they want. These issues are important not just within councils but across the whole social care system – including regulators, the general public, politicians – and from experience this cultural shift is the toughest challenge of them all. Many current providers are exploring real solutions to their particular challenge and it is interesting to see how they are contributing significantly, usually where the local authority system has let go of its old fashioned 'commissioner/provider' superiority mindset, and has embraced collaboration and partnership that respects differences in roles but knows that all parts of the system have an important role to play.

I am immensely grateful to each and every contributor to this handbook – each of whom in their own special and distinctive way have shared how they have explored creating a world where people are offered, with no agenda, possibilities and choices that they can freely choose from. I am particularly thankful to those contributors who in doing so have given very personal accounts of their lives, not just their professional experience. But to each one, I am very lucky to have met you, been inspired by you, and been able to learn from your contribution.

My enduring hope is that this volume plays a small but noticeable part in encouraging people in all parts of the social care system to rethink how the system works, and that as a consequence those people who need to support to get on with their lives will more closely live the life they want and have a right to hope for.

A wise man once said, 'Never lose your sense of outrage!'

Chapter 1

From carer to citizen leader

Tony Bennett

I came late to social care, and I came knowing nothing; it's only an accident of geography that I ever arrived anywhere. But come to social care I did, my wife and I, by now sure that there was something more seriously wrong with my parents than old age and a bit of forgetfulness. They both, of course, had Alzheimer's disease – that nasty, degenerative, person sapping evil that an aging population views with inevitability – there's no hope, and no hope of a cure for those currently suffering.

Having trod the path of misunderstanding, denial and eventual acceptance, we tried to do what my parents had told me I should do – never put them in a home. We contacted social services early on and a worker came to visit us at my parents' house. She was able to offer some home care, and perhaps a visit to a day centre. At this time my parents still had enough wits about them to know that a day centre never had been, and never would be for them; and my mother was still able to persuade herself that she was cooking meals and going about her household tasks with the same contempt for dirt and disorder as she had always had. The sad truth was that they were not eating properly, and the house was not as it always had been. But they still had the capacity at that point to refuse, and they did.

Time passed, 18 months or so, and the situation deteriorated to the point where my wife and I were unable to not intervene. They had run out of heating oil and forgotten the need to buy it. Dad had omitted to put water in the car radiator and the engine had seized up. They were shopping only randomly, and were only eating the biscuits, crisps and yogurts that we used to leave them.

We had a further meeting with social services, and soon after a microwave and freezer full of microwave meals was delivered – the modern day replacement for the care and compassion of meals on wheels. With this came homecare, a 20-minute visit at random times to prepare them both a meal, and an abortive attempt at a day centre – they were to be picked up by the special bus at 9am on Wednesday, or whenever, and my parents, of course, were not outside waiting – they had no idea what day it was, never mind the hour.

They actually went once – my wife and I had decided that we needed to get them out of the house together so that we could tackle some of the things that had been neglected around the house. The worst of it was in the kitchen where the carpet needed to be removed to restore some semblance of hygiene, and the fridge sanitised to a reasonable state. I actually took them, and brought them back. I never inflicted that alien experience on them again.

Homecare brought about its own challenges – they were sometimes refused entry; often my parents said they had already eaten, sometimes, regrettably, no one came. I learned later of the differences between agency homecare, and that which is provided by the council, pity we never had the chance to experience the latter.

More time passed. The phone calls from concerned neighbours and the evidence before our eyes when we visited told us that we needed to get my mother to a place of safety – she was walking up a main road on a regular basis to get the bus home, and the relationship between her and my father had broken down. I think he had hit her (unthinkable) and she was a clear danger to herself and to a lot of motorists on a very busy road.

I called a social worker, we called a doctor, and I managed to persuade my mother to let me take her to hospital. She never came home, and is in a care home, where I know she does not want to be.

My father was home alone, and my wife and I made sure that we travelled to see him every day. By now social services were coming twice a day, once in the morning and once at lunchtime to prepare some toast and a microwave meal at lunchtime. However, their times of attendance were different each day, and my father ate little of the food that they prepared for him. He wanted someone to sit and eat with him as he had been accustomed to, not to drop it in front of him on a tray and leave him to it.

In the middle of 2006 the job that I enjoyed changed when the parent company was taken over and most of the purpose of my position stripped away until redundancy was the inevitable result. My wife and I decided then that a fortuitous situation had arisen, and that we should now care for my father full-time. This we did, travelling the miles over the Lincolnshire dyke bounded roads until we realised that it was not working for us, or for him. We resolved that we needed him to be with us, or us with him. We let out our house and moved in with him in April 2007.

My first move was to dispense with all of the services that had been provided by the care agency. I deemed them totally inappropriate, of poor quality, and of limited value to my father for all of the time he had received them. And to make matters worse, my father had been contributing financially to this.

It's here that my real involvement with social services began. My wife had telephoned them to see what they could offer in our new circumstances – they said we could have more of the same: homecare, day centre, microwave meals. My wife accepted that we were on our own; I did not and later rang again to say that I would not be compartmentalised, or pigeonholed, and wanted a dialogue with a social worker to establish what help they could offer to us as we were. As there was no box on the form for someone like me, I was told that they would get someone to ring me.

I too thought at that point that we were on our own. I had done the rounds of the agencies and charities and had gathered a little bit of money, a lot of sympathy, and a modicum of emotional support. The call from the social worker was unexpected, and for me was to be a life-changing event. He said to me he would like to come and see us as he was working on a pilot project that he thought we might be interested in. He was, of course, the individual budget project worker, and when he came he explained that he was doing pilots for a project that was looking at delivering social care in different ways. He would be able to offer my father cash for his care, to be spent meeting objectives for him, which we would define in a support plan.

At last, something I could make sense of – I had written business plans, and was familiar with managing events, and budgeting and organising – this felt like coming home. It also sounded too good to be true. My scepticism and cynicism based on years of others promising the earth and delivering little had resulted in a very unhealthy, jaundiced regard for promises made by people who said that this would really be in our interest. Individual budgets have been many things to many people – as well as being good for my father, they also treated my jaundice, and thereby made me a little less cynical.

For my father, the interventions we undertook affected the quality of his life in a positive way, both directly and indirectly, because the respite care we had budgeted for was good for us. For me, a switch had been turned on, it seemed like somebody had accepted the mediocrity of the current provision of social care, and was trying to make it easier for people to live a better life. Regrettably, my father contracted an infection, and the years of care that we had planned to give him dwindled to months before we could no longer manage him and he went the inevitable route of hospital, care home and funeral parlour. That sounds very matter of fact – for myself, my wife and family, it was. We had mourned his passing over the time his mind had dissolved in front of us. My mother remains in a care home at the time of writing.

During that time before my father contracted an infection we had used the budget to enable him to spend time at my mother's care home, sometimes precious time when there was a mutual recognition, and they would walk together hand in hand, others when the only benefit to my father was a lunch out, and some time with different people. We used the respite care to have a weekend off to attend the air show at RAF Waddington. My father went to the home, we boarded the dogs, and the heavens opened and the air show was cancelled – carers' luck.

He had respite care to enable me to attend my first major event in Manchester. We never did have the planned time where someone from the Alzheimer's Society would come and sit with my father. They were unable to get a retired forces officer, who had volunteered, CRB checked quickly enough. My thoughts about that are completely unprintable.

I want to say something at this point about support planning. I have already said that preparing plans had been a part of my working life, and I approached writing a support plan from a similar standpoint. The consequence of this was that I expected that I would be challenged, as I had by customers and employers, about my words and figures. In the vernacular, I had expected my plan to have been given a 'good going over'. Because of this I wanted to be very sure that every word and figure could be justified.

Perhaps it was arrogance, but I considered that I knew with a degree of certainty what my father would have written had he been able so to do. I therefore decided to write the plan in the first person, as if he had actually written it. I was constrained then by only writing what I could demonstrate and could justify, so my plan had anecdotes from his current life, which I thought would ring true with anyone involved in dementia. I used photographs to illustrate what he had done, where he had lived, and how mum and he, and me when I was younger, had lived our lives together.

I tried to paint a picture of my father the man, not incapacitated by his illness, but in the fullness of his life. I hoped that by doing this the interventions that we organised would be seen as being in a continuum, in their rightful place, and grounded in the life that he once lived.

I learned much later about person-centred language and about knowing the person. The support planning workshops that I now facilitate are rooted in this experience, and are enhanced by the reading, learning and experiences in which I have been involved. There is more on this later.

The project worker and I formed a warm working relationship, and very soon I was involved in telling my father's individual budget story to a wide range of audiences, in a variety of media. I attended events and discovered that what I thought was actually

a good thing was being trialled in other geographical locations, and there were others, equally as fired up by this. I was invited to attend a Citizen Leaders Academy at Loughborough, where I received a very rapid initiation into a world of disability where individuals had triumphed over circumstance, which in my life to date I had no concept of.

We jointly learned about the history of self-directed support, about it being user-led, not government-led, and we listened to stories and created newspaper headlines about how the media might portray some of the things people were spending their budgets on.

For me, the cost and what folk were doing with their money came an irrelevant last to the life changing experiences that those sometimes pitifully small amounts of money were making in their lives. I was converted. Evangelists from St Paul to Billy Graham have gone through this Damascus Road experience. Converts need a community in which to thrive and grow, and I found that in those brief moments spent with other citizen leaders, especially those who were overcoming the barriers to citizenship that able bodied and minded people and organisations erect for their own self-serving interests. Also, I was in the company of like-minded individuals in Lincolnshire County Council social services, and the mental health teams, and I thank them for their passion and support.

My life to date had been spent primarily in business, though I also have a postgraduate teaching qualification and unhappy memories of 'teaching practice' as it was once called. I had worked as a business adviser and consultant, and managed companies, people and projects. I had the distinction of opening, as manager, a brand new B&Q store in Grimsby, which in those long ago days, was the first major retailer in the town to have an electronic point of sale system. This background had given me skills, which together with the expert by experience status I had acquired, enabled me to do two things – further my advocacy for self-directed support, and earn enough money that I should not need to return to regular full-time employment, which I had frankly had my fill of.

At the time of writing I feel like a sports fan given a job as a sports journalist or commentator. Actually, it's more than that because I see my efforts having a real influence on the way that personalisation and transformation is effected – my working life has a useful purpose and I get paid for it.

Initially I had some small pieces of paid work, and was then able to help planning and facilitating some training events. A contact sent me details of some national work that the Department of Health were undertaking. I expressed an interest in this, was interviewed and selected to work with citizen leaders, co-facilitating two co-production projects on resource allocation and outcome focused reviews. I deliver support planning workshops, and am developing other workshops that I think will add genuine value, and generate income for myself and my family.

I will devote the rest of this chapter to some observations about the work I currently undertake, and progress along the journey of transformation, which all of us involved in any way in adult social services are making.

My first observation is about co-production. It seems strange that we need a new buzzword to define a very simple process – involve your customers (I did say I came from a commercial world) in all of those things that affect them and the result will be better. Good retailers know this, and sometimes believe and demonstrate it. Good social services departments are adopting it; others are being forced into it. Whatever the route, the arrival is defined by better outcomes. I learned long ago of synergistic relationships, where the whole is greater than the sum of the parts. In an environment of openness and trust, the results that can come from users of services, their carers and families, working together with councils, are both eye opening and eye watering.

Working in real partnership, barriers to citizenship stripped away, social services doing for people, not to people, service users understanding the genuine not made up constraints councils are subject to – that is the route to efficiency, money saving, and genuine customer satisfaction all at the same time. I hear as I write, Lord Laming echoing my words – just get on with it!

'You are articulate, assertive, and able to get the best for your parents' is a phrase that has often been put to me. Usually followed by 'what about those who aren't as lucky as them?' My response to this is now standard – my parents are/were most certainly not lucky, followed by a comment about social workers being paid to help the most vulnerable in society, or had I got that wrong. I hear about lack of time, about lack of training, about lack of resources. All of this, to me, speaks of a culture that has for too long taken away from people the ability to do the job they were trained for. It also speaks of organisations that are poorly managed, or not managed at all in the traditional sense, of taking people to task over their shortcomings, and of departments that may be unmanageable. The flip side of this is those Damascus Road experiences that workers have had, which are largely and regrettably unreported and uncelebrated. I have mentioned my local council already. People can look at the evidence in terms of case studies and reflect on what has happened in the mental health trust again in the east of Lincolnshire, where some of the most vehement doubters were won over by just giving the process a chance. On the way they helped a good number of people have better lives – more of this later. James, whose story you can read on the personalisation website (http://www.dhcarenetworks.org.uk/Personalisation/Stories/

?parent=2738&child=4545) says that the process of getting an individual budget was cathartic for him in helping improve his mental health. It was also cathartic for the team who work with him, and offers hope for the future.

I would like to finish by referring back to support planning, as it is also relevant to the time/attitude debate. I regard getting the support plan as right as possible as being pivotal to the overall success of the journey for recipients of a personal budget. Anecdotal evidence I have collected whilst listening to people confirms this. To write a good support plan requires knowledge of the person, and of what is important to and for them. If people write their own plans, the first part is obvious, the second, without a guided thought process, is more challenging. My experience is of writing a plan for a person who did not know themselves. Going forward, it seems certain that the law will be changed to allow direct payments to be made to third parties on behalf of potential recipients for whom a personal budget is appropriate, but for reasons of capacity are not entitled to the direct payment of it.

In these circumstances we had better be certain that we are acting in the very best interests of those we seek to support – knowing the person here is of paramount importance if we are to demonstrate that best interest. This is a process that will take time to complete. However, if we invest the time at the front end of the process, the savings in both time and process as the journey unfolds will be the benefit reaped.

The challenge we face is to help people have better lives – this informs the way I want to go forward. It's been said of consultants that they only tell you what you already know. I call myself a citizen leader and I tell myself that the benefit of the changes in adult social care is best measured in those compelling stories of lives changed.

I came late to social care – it's already better than when I first found it, and has the potential to be transformed beyond recognition for the better.

Chapter 2

Personalisation and housing

David Abbey

Few choices in life are as important as where we live. So for personalisation to truly become a reality, the issue of housing must be addressed. This chapter explores the ultimate expression of personalisation – home ownership. It also explains a unique solution that enables people with a disability to really take control of their lives, buying a home of their own using only the benefits that they're entitled to.

Home really is where the heart is

Where we live, what we live in, who we live with and what kind of life our 'living' supports – these choices lie at the heart of most of our lives. They're choices that we often take for granted, so why shouldn't people with a disability enjoy the same rights? In our current social care system there are far too many examples where the environment that someone lives in is out of their control, failing to represent their choices or wishes. A truly transformed social care system must urgently challenge this kind of decision-making.

The current system segregates people who need support, channelling them into residential care, supported living (where they haven't necessarily chosen where they live or who they live with) and supported housing schemes (through supporting people finance) that puts their housing at risk if the support doesn't work or isn't what they want.

A personalised social care system needs to stop creating marginalised solutions to people's housing needs and advocate for proper access to mainstream housing choices through mainstream routes. It's not sufficient that we argue successfully for the building of shared ownership blocks of flats for instance – that may be an improvement but it's still constraining choice. What we need to be able to offer is the kind of support and assistance that enables people to act freely in the housing market like anyone else – without discrimination on the grounds of disability, age or ill health. Sounds too good to be true? It isn't. And it's already happening for hundreds of people.

MySafeHome has championed this right to access to mainstream housing for over a decade and it can be done for people on very low incomes with little chance of employment and none of the capital that is usually required to secure and maintain a house.

How do you and I buy a house? First of all we make decisions about who we want to live with, and where we want to live, we dream about what it might look like, where it might be. Then we bump into the reality of the market where usually our 'dream home' doesn't exist or is far too expensive. We make a shortlist, visit our most favoured options, and get into negotiations, having made inevitable compromises along the way.

This is the process that must be made available to people who need support to get on with their life and who want to explore the possibility of home ownership. What's traditionally stood in the way? First, there's very little help for disabled people who want to buy their own home. Second, mortgage lenders have been very reluctant to lend to disabled people with low incomes or a total reliance on state benefits. Third, there's been a lack of knowledge in local authorities – both housing and social care departments – which has led to disabled people being channelled down the marginalised, segregated route already described.

As a result, only a persistent few have managed to buy their own home. It's clear that many more people, given the opportunity, would like to explore this possibility. This includes people living in residential care, people living with parents or other relatives, young adults growing up, people living with older carers who are worrying about the future, people who have been moved away from their place of birth or their community and who want to move back to where they are known.

Of course home ownership is only one of a range of housing options for disabled people, but it's vitally important that it's open and accessible. 70% of housing stock in England is in the owner occupier sector. Without access to this, disabled people's housing choices will be hugely constrained.

Estate agents tell us that location is everything. For many people who need support to live their lives, location is even more important. Access issues in terms of transport, shops, neighbours and friends can be crucial. Some people will need very quiet locations, others will want busier, livelier spots. Housing is as individualised a choice as any that we make in our lifetimes – and much more important than most other decisions we get to make.

So, the challenges involved in personalisation and housing are as clear as the need for this form of freedom of choice. Now let's look at the solution.

Personalisation: Practical thoughts and ideas from people making it happen   © OLM-Pavilion 2009

Shared ownership explained

Shared ownership is a concept developed in the 1980s to help people who couldn't afford to buy their own home outright because of soaring property prices. It doesn't mean that people have to share their house – though they can choose to do so. Most shared ownership schemes work through housing associations who buy or build a property, then enable someone to buy a proportion of it (between 25% and 75%) and pay rent on the remainder. Shared ownership offers security – you can decide how long you live in your home. It costs less than full ownership and no deposit is needed for the purchase. In some cases, the housing association will be responsible for maintenance. It also provides an opportunity for families who can (and want to), to help buy the property – ie. it's a method through which parents who are getting older and who want to create long-term security for their family member can do so – if they have the means.

There are three types of shared ownership.

1. General needs shared ownership. This is commonly known as New Build HomeBuy and is funded by the government through housing associations. These are generally marketed towards working people on modest incomes. Repairs and maintenance are usually the responsibility of the homeowner, which can be a problem for disabled people who have less chance of building up capital.

2. Shared ownership for disabled people. This is commonly known as HOLD – home ownership for people with long-term disabilities. Again, this is funded by the government through housing associations. This is a more flexible scheme than NewBuild. For instance, it allows housing associations to buy homes through the open market using an estate agent. The government provides some finance to the housing association, which keeps the rent low. The lease requires the association to be responsible for repairs and maintenance, covered by a service charge, which is eligible for housing benefit. The disadvantage of this scheme is that relatively few housing associations have so far applied to the government for money to fund it.

3. Shared ownership using family or trust fund. This is commonly known as family funded shared ownership and is funded by parents, a trust fund or other sources. The money is given to a housing association as a loan – this replaces the money normally provided by the government. No interest is paid, the loan is used to purchase the housing association's share of the property, the loan is repaid on the sale of the property with a proportionate share in any growth, and this loan keeps the rental amount low. These schemes always have a suitable lease for disabled people. The advantage of this scheme is that it can provide housing at much less than market cost. However, a minimum investment of £30k is required.

Overcoming the obstacles – turning hopes into homes

One of the main blocks to home ownership for someone with a disability is finding a mortgage provider who's willing to lend to people on low incomes or reliant on benefits. A second problem is that many benefits agencies are not familiar with the relevant regulations and need support and assistance to understand the system that they are administering.

To overcome these challenges (and several more besides) MySafeHome developed a strong working relationship with a stable mortgage lender (willing to offer 100% mortgages) and formulated a process that's stood the test of time, helping hundreds of disabled people buy a home of their own. Here's how it works.

1. Mortgage application – an expert adviser ensures the viability of the proposal by assessing the potential buyer's financial situation and current benefit entitlement.
2. Solution presentation – the expert adviser visits the potential buyer and other family members/their circle of support to explain the details of the scheme.
3. Mortgage accelerator – the adviser provides assistance in completing the mortgage application and collating the supporting paperwork. This greatly increases the likelihood of receiving a mortgage offer at the first attempt.
4. Mortgage lifetime tracker – through a particular mortgage product that's been negotiated with a particular lender, full protection is provided against interest rate rises across the full term of the mortgage. The mortgage offer is thoroughly checked by the expert adviser before exchange of contracts.
5. Mortgage payment support – the expert adviser ensures that mortgage payments are made by the benefits agency as soon as possible and ensures that the homeowner does not receive any mortgage arrears letters. For a minimum of three years, the payments will be checked and reinstatement support will be provided if needed.
6. Legal assistance – in the unlikely event that the benefits agency refuses to make the mortgage payment, additional support can be provided including requesting a formal review of the case and even representing the buyer at a tribunal if necessary.

Here's an example of the potential figures involved in a shared ownership scheme.

Property value	£160,000
60% sale	£96,000
40% rent	£150 per month
Service charge	£130 per month
Mortgage on £96k	£450 per month paid by support for mortgage interest (SMI) direct to building society
Rent	£150 per month paid by housing benefit direct to housing association
Service charge	£130 paid by housing benefit direct to housing association
There is a home purchase fee amount of approximately £3,000, but after that the monthly housing cost could be FREE to the homeowner.	

Of course, as with any mortgage, there's an approval process and not everyone will be successful. There are other issues to be aware of too, especially in relation to work. Disabled people who have paid work of more than 15 hours a week may not get help towards their mortgage payments (SMI benefit). This doesn't mean that they can't get a mortgage but it may limit the amount they can borrow. Many disabled people in work have been supported in the way described above to buy their own home.

Home ownership may not be suitable for people who are currently unemployed but are thinking about taking up employment, as paid work may then cancel out benefits and make the mortgage unaffordable – this is just one of the many benefit 'traps' in our current system. If people are thinking they may get paid work they'll need to take this into account when considering how large a mortgage they can afford.

There are also important capacity issues to consider. Home ownership involves contracts. The appointment of a deputy via the Court of Protection is one route that can be followed to assist people who may not understand the meaning of their contract. The appointment of a deputy enables a family member or someone else who is trusted and has legal capacity to sign the relevant paperwork on behalf of the homeowner but, crucially, the property will always belong to the disabled person.

So that's the theory. How does it all work in reality? Here are a couple of case studies that clearly demonstrate the benefits that home ownership delivers.

Trevor's story, Leicester

'I encountered a great deal of difficulty in the social environment in which I was being housed,' recalled Trevor, the painful memories of those days still clearly felt. *'Unfortunately, that meant that my mental health state completely deteriorated.'* In fact, Trevor was told that he would spend the rest of his life on a dizzying cocktail of medication to keep his condition under control.

There followed a frustrating period of consultation with psychiatrists, carers, social services and Trevor's local council – all of whom agreed that he needed to be moved somewhere else, but where? There simply wasn't a suitable answer, except to be moved to a high-rise block of flats with, as Trevor notes ominously *'...all of the inherent social problems. It wasn't just affecting my mental health state it was affecting me physically'.*

Then the possibility of home ownership was flagged up and Trevor's world began to change. *'Suddenly I thought, hold on, there's light at the end of the tunnel. And that I had to hold on to. I had to believe that there would be that light.'* Working closely with Advance Housing and MySafeHome, Trevor found his dream property and secured the mortgage that he needed to buy his share.

Trevor picks up his story. *'Now? I've come off the majority of my medication, I don't suffer so many panic attacks. I'm not afraid of people around me and I'm more at ease with myself, more comfortable with who I am and where I am.'* This turnaround is totally at odds with the future that Trevor once faced. *'I'm a different person to who I was five years ago, completely changed and that's down to living in accommodation that I wanted to live in, in an area I chose to live in and not being dictated to by a council or housing association saying this is what we've got, take it or leave it.'*

While the details of the unique shared ownership scheme were, as Trevor noted, *'explained in great detail, that made it very easy to follow, very easy to understand and in actual fact, negated many of the questions that you were going to ask'.* Difficulties came from perhaps unexpected quarters.

'We've encountered difficulties where the support team ie. your social workers, your carers, all thought these schemes were too good to be true. In many cases now it's not the client who has a problem with the scheme, or understanding it or its benefits, it's getting through to a lot of the support workers that this is a very feasible and acceptable scheme. It does support people, give them independence and many of us have made leaps and bounds in our well-being and find ourselves part of the community again – being included, not excluded.'

Seeing Trevor today, looking round his immaculate home and blooming garden, it's hard to imagine that he was effectively written off and destined to spend the rest of his life in some form of care facility, on a range of medications. Now, as well as living independently, he's contributing to his community through voluntary work and looking forward to life once more. It might just be bricks and mortar, but to Trevor, a home of his own is much more than that. It's hope.

Jake's story, Doncaster

Like many young people of his age Jake had been enjoying life at college, becoming more and more independent. However, the end of his studies brought with it the inevitable return to the family home and, potentially, an end to the incredible progress that he'd been making.

As his mum Janet put it, *'It seemed as if he'd gone backwards in a way from being independent'*. Jake's local council had found a couple of properties that he could move to but, in both cases, the locations were unsuitable, either too far from home and the friends and family he knew or right in the town centre on a really busy road. Janet leapt into action and made some enquiries, discovering that Jake could not only choose his own property but also become a joint owner with his very own mortgage, covered entirely by existing benefits.

Once again, as so many potential homeowners and their families admit, they were a little sceptical. As Janet recalls, *'It seemed too good to be true, we just couldn't believe it would all work out as well as it did'*. But, following a meeting with an experienced adviser, she was completely reassured. Jake found his ideal property, the mortgage was arranged and his benefits covered the monthly costs. Now he's happily living as independently as any other young person.

'For us it has certainly given us peace of mind that we know that for the foreseeable future Jake can be living here. He's secure and when we're not around, if he needed to, he could buy the house outright,' says Janet. *'I just can't believe how well it's all worked. I'm absolutely delighted that it's all worked so seamlessly.'*

MySafeHome

Established in 1997, MySafeHome is the UK's leading provider of help and support for disabled people who want to buy their own home. In the intervening years they've helped hundreds of people (with everything from mild learning difficulties through to complex mental and physical health needs) turn hopes into homes. Through their MySafeHome Alliance they also offer a comprehensive consultancy service that provides organisations (housing associations, PCTs, care providers and local

authorities) with the support that they need in order to make home ownership for people with a disability a reality.

For more information, visit www.mysafehome.info, email enquiries@mysafehome. info or call 08000 121333 for further details and a free DVD featuring interviews with previous buyers and their families.

Personalisation: Practical thoughts and ideas from people making it happen   © OLM-Pavilion 2009

Chapter 3

Commissioning in a personalised system: experiences from the Cornwall Change Team

Geoff Baines, Sam Sly and Jo Hogg

In July 2006, the Healthcare Commission and the Commission for Social Care Inspection published their joint report into services provided to people with a learning disability by Cornwall Partnership NHS Trust. The report of the investigation highlighted significant failures of the NHS Trust and other agencies and led to Cornwall Partnership NHS Trust being placed under special measures. The special measures were lifted in March 2008 following significant improvement and a step change in culture for the individuals affected within the report.

The joint investigation was in relation to 200 people who received care and support from the NHS Trust, the majority of whom had historic links to old long-stay hospitals, this had contributed to their situation where they were excluded from accessing mainstream adult social care services. This is in the context of the general population of Cornwall of approximately 520,000 people and approximately 1,300 adults with a learning disability known to adult social care services.

The joint investigation report was highly critical of the agencies involved and the scale of the findings and recommendations have had a significant impact at national level. As a direct result of these findings, the Healthcare Commission undertook a national audit of services provided by NHS trusts and independent hospitals to people with a learning disability. The findings of this national audit identified a wide range of common concerns regarding the quality of traditional support for people with a learning disability (Healthcare Commission, 2007). In addition, the investigation findings regarding a large number of unregulated and unregistered care services provided by the NHS trusts contributed to the Commission for Social Care Inspection publishing its policy and guidance assessing whether a care service needs to be registered. Furthermore, based on the experiences of the Cornwall investigation, the Healthcare Commission along with the Commission for Social Care Inspection and the Mental Health Commission undertook a joint audit of commissioning specialist learning disabilities services for people with complex needs across 10 sites within England (CSCI, HC & MHAC, 2009). The contemporary standards used within the audit highlighted further issues of great concern regarding the extent to which commissioners have been able to identify the needs of local populations and implement commissioning systems that allow people to have control of their individualised support that they may choose.

The principles that continue to be the cornerstone of social equality are described within *Valuing People Now: The delivery plan* (Department of Health, 2009). This consistently clarifies expectations of equal rights, independence, control and inclusion and concerns the transformation of adult social care into a personalised world through Putting People First (HM Government, 2007). This highlights the importance of placing leadership within the local authorities. The future of personalisation is a running theme through health and social care policy. Another clear example of this within Valuing People Now is the target for the NHS to transfer social care resources to local authorities. Within the existing guidance for this, clear statements are made about the expectations of the elements of contemporary commissioning, which it is evident from the audit and investigations described above are not in operation in many areas of the country. The contemporary commissioning guidance (Department of Health, 2008) states:

- people should be supported to live in their own homes, with tenancies or owning their homes if they wish to do so
- people should receive support as close to home as possible
- people should have control over the funding, services and support they receive
- that the most appropriate service responses will be individually designed and tailored, rather than simply providing services in group or institutional settings
- the core of commissioned services should be to support people to live full and active lives, with health interventions promoting positive health to support people accessing life opportunities in their community
- people will not be living as inpatients unless undergoing active assessment and treatment
- for people with very complex needs, health services are commissioned in partnership with local authority commissioned support to address their specific health needs
- an increase in the number of people in paid work.

It is clear that contemporary commissioning must be based in values and principles of personalisation, choice and control. As with many areas throughout the country that are at the mid point of a transformation process into a whole new world of

personalisation, Cornwall needed to support people to move from NHS campus accommodation using contemporary commissioning at a time when the remainder of its systems and services were operating using a traditional model.

This chapter illustrates examples of how the change process has been applied in Cornwall for agencies and those individuals and families subject to the joint investigation.

The investigation concerned 36 people with a learning disability who had been living within four small specialist learning disability hospital institutions as inpatients, a majority of whom had lived there for many years. At the time of the investigation, the environments were impoverished, inappropriate and for some of the people concerned, there was a catalogue of allegations of abuse. In addition, there were a further 163 people living in 43 houses across Cornwall, which were unregistered and unregulated and where care and support was provided by the local NHS trust. Most of the people have lived in these houses since they were set up some 15 years previously. The houses were referred to as supported living services and were considered as trailblazing when originally set up as these were an alternative to traditional residential care.

The close scrutiny provided by the joint regulators and the Department of Health led to an unprecedented level of priority within the local health and social care agencies who all confirmed their commitment to implement the improvements required. However, the speed and scale of change required could not be met by the existing agencies alone at that time and therefore a team of people with contemporary up-to-date experience was brought in to support local agencies and was referred to as the 'Change Team'. The Change Team provided a facilitative role, dedicated leadership and experience and knowledge of up-to-date practice. It is important to note that health and social care agencies increased their capacity and skill over time and along with other local champions, carers and self-advocates, collectively, all played an important part in delivering the priority changes.

Leading a change programme

Leading a significant change programme presents many challenges where the aspirations for the new world of personalisation clash with the established traditional practice and experiences. It has also been important to remain steadfast when implementing change within organisations where tangible evidence of the known traditional services is perceived as presenting far less risk to organisations than less tangible, theoretical developmental policy.

Under these circumstances, it is easy to see how large organisations without clear leadership to reinforce a vision with a common goal such as personalisation, continue to reinforce traditional models of working. This is understandable where the skills of

the organisations have been well developed to maintain the here and now and are rewarded to do so by regulation and performance frameworks. This is the behaviour referred to as *'doing the wrong thing righter'* (Seddon, 2008).

Staying focused

Practical steps were therefore taken to map out the necessary work streams through a project management approach. The very clear focus throughout the time of the project was the desired outcome of *'citizenship for people'* (Duffy, 2007). A number of strategies were used in order to communicate the vision of citizenship and to support the growth of local leaders who could continue to model this. One of the successful methods was to establish a leadership group. The leadership group made it possible for new self-advocates and carer leaders to emerge and gain support alongside key senior leaders from health and social care organisations.

Values compass

One of the other successful tools developed by the team in order to support people to remain focused has become known as the values compass.

The direction finders for the compass are all the descriptors used to express the values we are aiming for, such as:

- citizenship
- inclusion
- choice
- control
- shifting power to people from organisations.

These values are our destination and although these tell us where we are headed, they do not describe what it will be like when we get there or what to look for. The compass is therefore valuable when in uncharted territory where the future is not clear and there are few traditional benchmarks to compare with. The powerful support it provides in these circumstances is that it clearly confirms plans of actions that are not compatible with your values, allowing you to discard them and justify to your many opponents why you should continue to this new world. A few key examples of challenges that have been faced where the compass has been of value are listed in **table 1**.

As **table 1** describes, the compass can discard proposed traditional approaches and therefore identify work streams for development.

Throughout the lifetime of the Change Team in Cornwall, there were a number of work streams underway simultaneously in order to provide the infrastructure and support to

Table 1

Proposed action traditional model	What would the compass tell you – contemporary values	Work streams to develop
All people should receive a local authority community care assessment and be moved from the hospital and placed in a community in group living/residential care.	Proposed action is traditional and service led, not personalised or based on the wishes, aspirations and talents of the individuals. Discard proposed action.	Individualised plans required eg. person-centred plan.
163 people living in 43 unregistered houses. The houses operate as un-registered residential care homes and therefore need to be registered as care homes.	Decision to register as a 'care home' is service led and not based on the choices of the individual. People need to be informed and empowered to make choices regarding their future. Discard proposed action.	Information and advice required on the pros and cons of both residential care and independent living. People to be empowered to make preferred choice.
Existing NHS trust provider to hand over the role of provider to an alternative organisation.	Service led approach. Traditional tendering approach – not individualised or based on the choice of individuals. Discard proposed action.	Develop a provider market of choice, brokerage support and a process of informed decision-making.

enable those concerned to have greater choice, control, independence and to feel in control. Some of the key work streams included:

- individual planning
- advocacy
- involving people and families
- developing a range of providers to choose from
- partnerships with providers
- commissioning
- revenue and capital funding
- developing a range of housing options
- stimulating housing supply
- resource allocation systems
- safeguarding
- decommissioning services
- transitional planning and support for people moving
- facilitating provider selection and decision-making
- monitoring quality.

The wide range of actions and developments that took place within Cornwall leading to the lifting of the special measures placed on Cornwall Partnership NHS Trust have included a great deal of activity, commitment and involvement of a wide range of organisations and many individuals. As a result, there are many success stories for individual people, however, there continues to be a significant amount of work to do to embed changes into the mainstream for local people. Despite this, of all the successes there have been, some examples of the strands of work that will be of interest in this personalisation story include the importance of individualised planning, working in partnership with providers, people and their families, and developing a menu of choices.

Individual planning

Up until the inspection, the planning that had taken place around the individuals who needed to move on from both the hospitals and the supported living services had not directly involved families or the people themselves. Professionals had been making decisions about people's futures based on an out-of-date medical model of disability.

Different plans had been floating around that varied in quality and accuracy, some plans gave information about someone's health needs or perhaps something about how they communicated but there was no overall picture or sense of the person. This patchy information meant that any future plans around someone's home and support were at best 'guess work' and at its worst dangerous assumptions that could misinform and shape someone's future life. Without this in-depth knowledge about

individuals, professionals quickly slipped into making arbitrary decisions for them such as, 'Peter and Ian should live together because they tolerate each other.'

Based on this level of information it was not possible to inform housing and support providers of people's wishes and needs and move forward with the planned hospital closures.

The Change Team asked Doreen Kelly, director of Partners for Inclusion in Scotland to come and urgently support the planning process. Doreen's organisation supports people with learning disabilities, mental health issues and people with complex needs to live fulfilling lives in their own homes. Some of the people they support have had big reputations and labels of challenging behaviour. The success of her organisation stems from their individualised approach to offering a support service and its commitment to really learning to listen to people. They ensure that they have a real understanding of someone's story (that they know the whole person and everything that is important to them) through a person-centred process called individual service design. They support 45 people by providing 45 quite separate, individually tailored services.

Doreen trained a number of social workers, as well as delivering a series of workshops for existing staff, advocates, families and support providers in order to explain this new approach and the values underpinning it.

Designing an individual service is a process in which the person and all the people who know them well are brought together to help them think about their life so far and what their future life could be like. The facilitator's role is to draw out the fine detail from everyone and really explore the person's story. The facilitator must 'dig deep' and be prepared to ask some difficult questions. The process inevitably reveals the gap between life as it is and how it should be, and for some families and staff in Cornwall this was a painful experience.

Richard Bow remembers how difficult it was for him and his wife to listen to other people talking about their daughter Ellie:

'We realised that other people had got to know Ellie better than we did. They saw her every day and we didn't. I was not convinced that moving was the right thing for her as she'd lived in the same place for such a long time. But as we talked through the day and everyone who knew Ellie had their input, we started to see a different picture.'

Richard's daughter Ellie had lived with other people who she didn't get on with for a long time. As a family there had been no choices in the early days and Richard remembers that as a parent, you thought you were lucky when a vacancy came up for

your child. Following her individual service design, Ellie moved into her own home with her own supporters, since then she has gone from strength to strength.

Richard says, *'Ellie is so much happier and is doing much more for herself. She used to use just a few words but her vocabulary is growing by the day, she now talks to people on the phone, which is something we never imagined was possible. Her seizures or "episodes" have decreased significantly and hardly interrupt her life now.'*

In order to help people see future possibilities, the Change Team facilitated Richard and a number of other parents to go on a study tour to Liverpool to see how other support providers were supporting people with learning disabilities. Duncan Craig also went along. His daughter Anna had also been living in a place that did not meet her needs, with people she would not have chosen to be with. Duncan's wife Eileen remembers Duncan coming back from Liverpool full of new ideas and optimism for Anna's future. However, despite more housing options and a choice of support providers being made available in Cornwall (as a result of the change process), Eileen still remembers having to fight hard to get Anna out of her existing service and into her own home. The idea of moving Anna was also an unknown risk:

'At the time I just did not know that anything new existed outside the NHS, therefore I was worried that Anna could lose everything. But meeting Sue Prior (from United Response) and with Duncan's constant commitment I could see that a new life was possible for Anna.'

'I seriously regret having left Anna in the (shared house) for so long but what options were there? Who chooses to live with a group of people on the basis of age or disability? Most of us, Anna included, want our own home and to be surrounded by people who genuinely care. To see Anna walking down the street, or shopping with one of her carers – most people will see a pretty, well dressed, happy young lady with a support worker in her own community with absolutely no sense of institutionalisation.'

Eileen says that previously Anna was unable to walk long distances or on uneven ground and she believes this had nothing to do with Anna's capabilities and everything to do with the 'deprivation of experience' Anna faced everyday.

Eileen recalls, *'Going for a walk was at times substituted for being taken out in a wheelchair. Anna can now walk long distances, manage uneven ground and can even get herself up the ladder of a swimming pool unaided. So much has been achieved in just 18 months; I now feel that Anna has a real future ahead.'*

Richard Bow says that it's hard for families to imagine things being better and that having the chance to really think about what made sense for Ellie through some

detailed planning made all the difference. He says, *'How Ellie had lived was the way it had always been done but once we started to really think about it we could see that it wasn't the right way for her to live'*.

Creating alternatives for people to choose from

Following the development of quality individualised planning and a growing understanding that it can be possible for someone who has previously lived in an institution to have an alternative to residential care group living, it became clear that there were few existing alternatives, as the provider market within Cornwall was dominated by registered care homes. As a result of the national publicity that went alongside the high profile investigation, the director of the Change Team was contacted by a number of registered residential care providers within Cornwall and further afield who were keen to raise awareness of the vacancies within their own establishments. This was alongside existing traditional commissioning tools such as residential care vacancy lists and various pricing tools that all served to reinforce the limited opportunities. However, with reference to the values compass, these were easily disregarded as they were neither compatible with personalisation nor appropriate, having no link to individualised aspirations or wishes for the people concerned.

It was therefore necessary to develop the market not only in relation to the number of choices of provider that there may be but more importantly, with the range of lifestyles of living opportunities such as adult placements, independent living, rented accommodation, shared ownership and sheltered housing.

Therefore, the Change Team supported the local authority commissioning team to develop a specification that could be used to attract new providers that was based on personalised support. The specification was developed in partnership with families and people who were very clear about expressing what were the most important elements for them. This included the following statements.

- *'The provider I choose must provide the support I want for as long as I want them to, it will be me that gives them notice.'*
- *'The provider agency must support my son to do what he wants to do. He hasn't got to fit in with what they want.'*
- *'The provider must have consistent staff and human resource policies to retain them and allow my brother to select and choose the supporters he wants not get the ones that he is given.'*

This new partnership developed with the commissioning team alongside people and families enabled a clear specification to be developed that formed the basis for advertising for new providers to express an interest in working in Cornwall. An initial advert created a higher than expected level of interest from new providers throughout the country.

With a range of interest stimulated, new providers were invited to meet with the commissioners and family carers and representatives of the 200 people concerned in a number of events facilitated by the Change Team, which were referred to as 'clarification forums'.

The clarification forums were open meetings for providers where families and people themselves gave very clear messages, along with commissioners explaining exactly what would be expected.

The commissioners were able to clarify the scale of opportunities there were in Cornwall for new providers and families, and people themselves were clear about the specification that they would be expecting. It is important to note that evidence from individual planning at this stage strongly indicated the desire that many had to move towards independent living with support, and as such, it was possible to provide a strong indication to new providers. Earlier clarification forums were well attended by local providers who had previously been providing traditional registered care services, however, a number of these providers chose to opt out of further involvement as the model of service they were currently providing was quite different to what was being highlighted within the new developing specification. Some memorable questions raised within the open meetings at that time included the following statements.

- *'How will you as commissioner guarantee that there will be enough work for us local providers if you are bringing in new providers from outside of Cornwall?'*
- *'If we provide this individualised support for people, will they still be able to use a day centre five days per week during the day.'*

The nature of some of these questions raised at the early stages highlighted the importance of the provider market being up-to-date with best practice and organised in a way that could meet the individualised world of personalisation.

It is important to note that providers that expressed an interest and accepted the service specification were also subject to an accreditation process. Families and people were central in this process, ensuring the new providers were of sufficient quality.

The role of commissioners had therefore been to facilitate the development of the provider market and ensure that the standards of the providers were acceptable and therefore at an accredited level, shaped by people and families. This was a quality bar that had to be reached by the provider and those who had reached that bar would be offered to individuals and families as one of a range of choices.

There is no doubt that the feedback given by providers highlighted the significant shift in the balance of power regarding decision-making. Nick Fripp, now head of service for learning disabilities in Cornwall and at the time working for the Brandon Trust reported how his experience of this process differed from traditional approaches. Examples of these comparisons are listed in **table 2**.

Table 2		
	Traditional block contract – tender	**Cornwall – individualised**
1	One commissioning process, purchasing services for a group of people with learning disabilities	A separate commissioning process for each person
2	Centrally controlled process	Centrally facilitated process with local control (most often in the hands of people and relatives)
3	Two key documents submitted to commissioners – provider appraisal information and tender submission	Individual submissions for each person who has short-listed the organisation
4	Key decisions made by senior commissioners from health and social services supported by input from selected family members and people who use services	Key decisions made by individuals themselves and relatives supported by commissioners from health and social services and advocates
5	Individual people and their needs to be supported were unknown to providers in any detail	Needs of each person are known and a detailed plan for each person required a response to their own 'individual service design' document
6	Commissioners' belief that a change of provider would deliver better services	Commissioners' belief that individual choice and control will deliver better services
7	The provider's organisational policies, strategy, and track record under scrutiny	The provider's approach to each individual under scrutiny. This scrutiny is carried out by individuals themselves or their relative advocate.
9	Each tender evaluated using common selection criteria	Every individual submission subject to the differing selection criteria of individuals/relatives/advocates
10	The provider communication priorities focused on commissioners and unions	The provider communication priorities focused on individuals and their families

Collaboration with providers led to a number of successful provider fairs where providers were able to set out their stalls and provide general information to people and families making enquiries. The provider fairs were often referred to as successful events attended by large numbers of people.

Although actual decision-making by individuals and families may not have taken place directly at the fairs, they clearly modelled the possibility that choices could be made from a number of providers and that the important people, those with decision-making power, were the people and families themselves.

Creating a budget

Personalised approaches generally require (not as an end, but as a means) the identification of a budget identified to the individual, not to a particular service. This was an important step required in Cornwall in order to affect real change.

Transparency for people and their families regarding the cost of their current support arrangements and any funding sources available, proved to be a key factor in demonstrating a shift of power and control from commissioners to people and their families with support from advocates if required. Knowledge of funding entitlement for people and their families immediately provides people with 'buying power'.

In order to establish a budget for people without a pre-existing resource allocation process being available, a simple approach to identifying funds for individuals based on levels of need, current funding allocations, and the impact of creating a support plan that would really support and sustain their lifestyle was developed. This approach was consistent with other early resource allocation systems developed elsewhere in the country at that time. This was an important step to take, to embed and confirm that the process of commissioning, planning and procurement was now going to be an individual one, not an aggregated one.

Partnerships with providers, people with learning disabilities and their families

Involving and empowering people and their families with information, advice, decision-making power and a co-ordinated process was a key work stream for the Change Team.

The Change Team in Cornwall developed a personalised decision-making process and worked with people with learning disabilities and their families/advocates to choose for themselves a support provider (domiciliary care agency) to replace their existing NHS provider. At the same time, the team worked with support providers to change their

traditional approach of courting and then selling their service to the local council and primary care trust, to selling their service to individuals – a much tougher job. No longer did providers negotiate with faceless statutory agencies about tenders, beds and block contracts for faceless customers, instead they had to sell themselves to real people with real buying power. Individual contracts were set up for each person and providers therefore were more accountable to the individual they were supporting.

Tim Jones, south west regional director for United Response said of the move from block to individual contracts:

'The trouble is, block contracts offer organisations a great big get-out clause when it comes to addressing the relationship inequalities that so often cast individuals and their families in the role of passive recipients, there at the behest of other people who decide what is best for them. The personalisation agenda which Cornwall has started to address demands that such inequalities are replaced with genuine partnerships; partnerships in which the individual, their family and nearest and dearest figure out with paid people how it needs to be with and for the individual – what's important to and for them.'

Lynn Toman, area director for Brandon Trust said about the individualised process:

'It was in individuals' front rooms instead of tendering to a group or a panel. It meant I met all the individuals that we now provide support to, instead of a small representative group as part of a target tender process.'

Individuals and their families wanted more than just value for money; they were interested in how the organisation was run, whether it was privately owned or a charity, how many people the organisation supported, the training available to staff, and how the people they met spoke to and treated their relative with a learning disability. All these factors played an important part in decision-making. Providers soon learned that people were not impressed by glossy brochures and rhetoric. They wanted concrete detail of how they would be supported to live the life they wanted to lead. And for some providers this was a welcome break from traditional processes.

Tim Jones said, *'I have never been a fan of the traditional commissioning process. It never seemed real to me. Slick presentations, glossy brochures, discussions about people reliant upon support services, as opposed to discussions with people, were exacerbated by the fact that often those present at such presentations knew next to nothing about the individuals concerned. None of us might have ever met the person, yet here we were making all-important decisions about them. And if that was not bad enough decisions would often be made on the basis of whose written, verbal and presentation skills came across best.'*

In Cornwall a decision-making process was developed that enabled individuals and their families to have as much support, and get as much information as they needed to make a decision about a new provider. This meant that information about the process and providers was made readily available and in easy-read formats. 'Meeting facilitators' were employed to support families and individuals. Provider fairs were put on and advocates were used if people lacked representation. Providers were invited to meet people and when they had narrowed their choice down to three potential providers, these three were asked to look at the person's support plan and budget and detail the service they would provide. Much energy, time and resources were poured into the decision-making process as it was felt that being able to choose was what was most important. Sandy Collington, mother of Rachel said, *'We hadn't had to make such important decisions for so long'.*

Many of the providers in Cornwall were setting up in the county for the first time; this was useful in three ways, first, because they brought with them a quality of practice that was limited in the existing market. Second, being new, the individualised processes being developed were accepted more readily than by providers who had already been established and functioning in the existing traditional domiciliary care market. Third, both providers and people with learning disabilities with their family were starting from the same place and were learning together.

Doreen Kelly from Partners for Inclusion trained providers in personalised approaches. This training helped providers to shift towards more person-centred services. Providers have said that what they have learned in Cornwall has influenced the development of other parts of their organisations around the country.

Another useful event that happened early in the process was that the providers were supported to set up a forum to support one another; sharing training, good practice, lessons learned and resources – this is something often lacking in a competitive marketplace. Lynn Toman said of this:

'There were many positive elements of the process in Cornwall. One of the main ones for me was the partnership working of the different providers. It's the closest I have worked and shared information with other service providers. I hope this continues as it can't be anything other than beneficial.'

Providers were able to gain 'strength in numbers' when it came to negotiating with commissioners. Issues could be resolved more quickly, learning and best practice could be shared and the cultural change towards personalisation was taken on more readily and whole-heartedly by all of them.

The people of Cornwall, both those with a learning disability and their families were not used to having a voice or making decisions and this was a major failing identified in the Health Care Commission investigation. Sandy Collington, mother of Rachel said, *'One of the many things I have learnt, in the past two years is to be able to speak out more, not for myself but for my daughter'.*

Families had, over the years, seen decisions about their loved ones' lives taken on by the staff supporting them – some felt this was good, others did not. Some had lost contact altogether. This process therefore enabled some family members to get back in touch with their relatives with learning disabilities for the first time in years.

People with learning disabilities and families reacted in different ways to being given the power of decision-making. Some were angry, or scared by the seeming enormity of the task, some felt that the decision-making was a statutory agency responsibility, some sadly did not see that even after the abusive situations that their relatives were found to be in, why things needed to change. The lack of good quality advocacy for those not lucky enough to have family engagement became apparent – especially self-advocacy support. This is something that is echoed around the country. Without this, resource effective decision-making is hampered considerably.

Quality of life

Given the scale of the transformation required by traditional health and social care commissioning, contracting and procurement systems to move to an individualised world, it is not surprising that those champions involved in leading this cultural shift will regularly encounter influential people who need evidence to convince them of the benefits of this approach.

Qualitative data shows overwhelming improvement to individuals who now have more control over their lives. Janet Snell, editor of *Learning Disability Today* magazine had the opportunity to meet several people and their families in Cornwall in their own homes who tell their own stories (see Snell, 2009).

Anna's story

When Anna was 19 she was living in a group home with four other young adults. They didn't get on particularly and there was no choice as to who lived there.

Her mother, Eileen Munday, says Anna and one other resident were the only mobile ones. *'Anna tended to go into people's bedrooms and interfere with their stuff, which got her into all sorts of trouble'.*

Things were ticking over but then a new manager took over the running of the home and it 'nosedived', says Mrs Munday.

'Anna was told she could only be taken swimming if the rest of the group wanted to go. The whole place started to lose its way.'

Anna's father Duncan went up to Liverpool and saw people with high support needs living in their own place. He says, *'Until I saw it with my own eyes I just didn't think it was possible. When I got back, I went to all the meetings about Anna and made a nuisance of myself. I was sure she would be better in her own space'*.

Now Anna is 30, she owns 53% of a house she has bought under shared ownership with Advance Housing; her life has been transformed.

'The staff where she used to live said she would find it really difficult to make the move. Well, she didn't. We brought her belongings over here and she just moved in,' explains her mother.

She has a staff team of five or six and they provide 24-hour one-to-one cover with an hour's overlap for a handover. United Response is the employer but Anna and her parents choose the staff.

When she was in residential care, staff gave Anna a wheelchair and she had little strength in her legs. But now she dashes from room to room and goes shopping and to regular swimming sessions with staff. Her parents describe her as, *'much happier. She doesn't get crotchety like she used to and she has grown a lot more confident'*.

Her mother says:

'At first we wondered "can we exist without NHS accommodation?" It was a very a scary process we had to go through to get where we are now. But it's working out well and it has really opened our eyes to the possibilities for Anna.

'She can't tell us what she wants but she can let us know what she likes. She's very aware now that she has choices!

'I just want people to know – this is not a pipe-dream and it's not a "Rolls Royce" service as some have described it. It's real and it can be done.'

Jodie's story

As part of the closure programme for Budock long-stay hospital in Falmouth, Golden Lane Housing bought a house with Jodie in mind. She wanted to be able to visit Truro and be near her mum, but *'not too close!'*

Jodie talks about her time at Budock as when she was 'inside'. *'People hit me and pulled my hair. They took my toys and broke them. I had a very bad time there.'*

She says that when she saw the house in Truro, she thought *'that's freedom'*. *'I liked it because it was quiet and peaceful. I moved in on 22 of October 2006.'*

'Now I go out and I do gardening, painting, and swimming. I am going to start walking with a group. In the house, I'm going to change the curtains – I would like a different colour.'

The support provider is Brandon Trust. *'It's good because there is always a member of staff here who helps me if I need it. Having your own place takes a bit of time to get used to. But I'm happy now.'*

Kerr's story

Kerr Moodie was one of 13 people living on an NHS campus at West Heath Hospital in Bodmin. Kerr's support worker, Helen Smith, describes West Heath as *'like living on top of each other. It wasn't ideal, so I showed Kerr an advert I saw in the paper about available housing. We thought it sounded like a good idea'*.

Kerr liked it as soon as he saw the estate agent's picture of the house and after clearing all the hurdles and formalities, he moved there in September 2007.

He says it feels *'very good'*. *'I have more space here.'*

Kerr has a job one hour a week cleaning in a pub restaurant. *'I'm paid £5.50 for my job and I get a free pot of tea! When I started I was doing cellar work but because I did it ok, now I keep the garden tidy and the car park. That's my job. And I get £20 a month pocket money.'*

Kerr likes shopping, camping and hiking. *'I like to meet my mum for a cup of coffee in Bodmin once a week.*

'I don't ever want to go back to West Heath. I've learned to cope on my own now. I put my washing on myself. I wash up. I make my bed. I help get the food ready.

'I sent the neighbours cards at Christmas and they ask me how I'm doing. The best thing about being here is the freedom of movement. It's my house – so I'm independent now.'

Michael's story

Michael moved into his own place in the village of Mabe in February 2008. He says his favourite things are cars and going to the pub. *'I like stirring the gravy. And doing the hoovering with the Henry. I put my clothes in the washing machine. And I like listening to the radio in my bedroom.'*

Susan, his support worker, has been with him for 19 years. She moved from his care home to join United Response so she could continue to work with him. *'I'm the only thing that has come from the old days into his new life.'*

She describes him as *'more confident'* now and able to make decisions for himself. *'Before it would always be a group decision to do something. Now that it's just him he has a lot more choices.*

'When he first moved I was saying to him all the time "do you want this or that?" But now he just says "I want that".

'At first the house was pristine as he kept cleaning it. But then he started to realise "this is mine" so it looks a bit more lived in these days! And he has started making changes around the house and buying new things.'

Susan adds, *'It's very much his place now. There was one time when we were cooking and the kitchen window steamed up so I opened it. And Michael said "it's too drafty" and he just closed it. I thought that was great'.*

Michael gets up in the morning when he wants to. Two days a week he goes to a craft circle. Then on Thursdays and Fridays it's either swimming, shopping, going for a walk or a trip on the train.

Susan says he gets a lot more exercise than he used to so he has lost weight. *'Before he was a bit of a couch potato. The good thing is we have built up a relationship of trust. We do a lot together but there's a male worker who does boy-type things with him.*

'In the care home he didn't really choose how he lived. There was definitely a mismatch with the other people he lived with. It led to frustration. By the end it wasn't the right placement for him. Now he is much more relaxed.'

Susan says that *'with the best will in the world, a care home with five clients and two staff on, we couldn't always meet everyone's needs all the time. If Michael said no to what was on offer we would leave him. But now Michael and I are one to one and we can do more things. It's better for Michael but it's also more rewarding as a worker.*

'I have seen a big change in him. And for the first time in a long while I really look forward to coming to work.'

His sister Wendy adds, *'When we were first told he was going to move out we thought "no way".*

'But it's totally changed his life for the better. He is far less stressed now. He likes to relax in his chair with his sweets at his side. In the home he would get agitated because people would take his sweets. Now he can leave them by his chair and know they will still be there when he gets back. His psoriasis has gone. He is 51 years of age and happy.'

Russell and Gerald's story

Russell Bevan and his brother Gerald were both living in a residential care home when one Christmas Russell came home for the holiday and said he wasn't going to go back.

His mother Pauline explains, *'He said "I want to move". His weight had gone down to six and a half stone and we realised there was a problem'.*

When his parents contacted the home, staff said that unless Russell went back they would give his place to someone else. *'We just said "go on then". So that was the end of that. They never wanted to know why he didn't want to go back.'*

His parents heard about shared ownership through the parents and carers group and after they were told that their sons qualified, they soon found suitable properties for each of them. In Russell's case the house was on the market for £185,000 but they negotiated the price down to £179,000. The family put in £7,400. Advance Housing bought it and shortly afterwards Russell moved in.

His brother Gerald has also now moved into his own place. Pauline says, *'At first we were against shared ownership. We had an image of them being in debt for £100,000. When you go in for a mortgage it's a very worrying time. You wonder whether the authorities will always pay for it. And you worry whether someone with limited capabilities will make a go of it.*

'But it's worked out well for Gerald and for Russell. They are both much more confident. Gerald is a different person. He didn't seem settled before and he didn't get on with some of the others in the house he shared. But now we have never seen either of them so happy.'

Conclusion

Here are some final thoughts from us, as authors, about our reflections now on this process.

- The skills of leadership and sustaining change that were required represent a significant shift from a majority of the professional skills in the traditional world. Leaders must be able to maintain their clarity of vision and commitment in the face of pressure to keep to traditional ways of working.
- This paradigm shift in the process of commissioning required a significant culture change and power shift and continues to need time to embed.
- There are debates to be had about whether to adopt a 'big effort, big bang' approach to change or adopt an incremental change process. In Cornwall, the former was required by the results of the inspection. In many ways, on reflection this helped to power through what otherwise may have been insurmountable obstacles. By its nature, incremental change evolved over time whereas this may be a less painful and smoother process for organisations, individual people may be prevented from significantly improved outcomes for important periods of their life.
- The process demonstrated that when people create individualised support plans, and have good quality information and advice and support for decision-making, this leads to significantly improved outcomes.
- In Cornwall, the change was engineered through a 'demand side revolution', which in hindsight proved much speedier than bureaucratic transformation from within the existing conventional system.
- There is immense value in creating true constructive partnership with providers, rather than the conventional competitive relationship engendered by standard tendering processes.
- Creating the shift to a personalised, individualised approach is not something that one person or one organisation can do alone. In Cornwall, there was input from people with learning disabilities and their families, an external change team, Care Services Improvement Partnership (CSIP), Valuing People Support Team (VPST), advocacy agencies, external experts, and all the statutory agencies.

Finally, once power is redirected to those that it should be with, and people accept their right to take control and make choices about their lives, expectations get raised, people grow stronger and they won't ever hand it back. Statutory agencies need to

learn this fast and stop being afraid. Once the shift of power takes hold the momentum takes on a life of its own and cannot be stopped. It was great to be still working with people six months after their initial choice of provider and observe them demanding the same individualised choice processes when it came to changing support provider second time around.

References

Commission for Social Care Inspection & Healthcare Commission (2006) *Joint Investigation into Services for People with Learning Disabilities at Cornwall Partnerships NHS trust*. London: Commission for Healthcare Audit and Inspection.

Commission for Social Care Inspection, Healthcare Commission & Mental Health Act Commission (2009) *Commissioning Services for People with a Learning Disability and Complex Needs*. National report of joint review. London: CSCI, HC & MHAC.

Department of Health (2008) *Valuing People Now: Transfer of responsibility for the commissioning of social care for adults with a learning disability from the NHS to local government*. London: Department of Health.

Department of Health (2009) *Valuing People Now: The delivery plan*. London: Department of Health.

Duffy S (2007) *Keys to Citizenship: A guide to getting good support for people with learning disabilities*. Birkenhead: Paradigm Consultancy and Development Agency.

Healthcare Commission (2007) *A Life Like No Other: A national audit of specialist inpatient health care services for people with learning difficulties in England*. London: Healthcare Commission.

HM Government (2007) *Putting People First. A shared vision and commitment to the transformation of adult social care*. London: The Stationery Office.

Seddon J (2008) *Systems Thinking in the Public Sector*. Axminster: Triarchy Press.

Snell J (2009) A silver lining. *Learning Disability Today* **10** (2) 22–25.

Chapter 4

Personalisation and providers
Micro providers

Sian Lockwood

Background

Micro enterprises (services delivered through five or fewer workers) are vital elements of a diverse market that provides real choice to people. However, the number of micro providers has fallen over the last five years as a result of the many barriers to setting up and sustaining a micro service, including regulations, legislation and commissioning practice designed for larger organisations.

The Department of Health has funded a three-year National Association of Adult Placement Services (NAAPS) project to stimulate the development of a range of tailored and innovative adult social care and other micro enterprises in order to provide real choice for individuals needing support to live and be part of their local community. The project identified and tested an effective business model that can be used to stimulate and support a vibrant local micro market. Learning from the project is being brought together in a practical guide for use by any local authority to build a thriving local market of micro providers.

The main focus of the last year of the project will be the testing of an adaptation of the agency model to provide kitemarking and a quality assurance service for micro enterprise. The learning from this will inform an addendum to the practical guide, which will address safeguarding and quality assurance issues and will be published in March 2010.

The project

The business model

The basic business model was developed in discussion with micro social care and support entrepreneurs and informed by learning from micro entrepreneurs across all sectors. It was designed to be a support agency, offering a range of services to existing and new micro providers as well as signposting people to other local sources of support and advice. It required a full-time co-ordinator with good local management support. At the start of the project there were clear expectations as to the main services that would be offered by the support agency.

Pilot areas

Clear criteria governed the selection of the two local authority pilot areas and the selection process ensured that the two pilot sites met all the criteria and were very different to each other. One pilot area, Oldham in the north west of England, is a small and urban metropolitan borough council, whilst the other, Kent in the southeast, is a large county council operating across 12 districts with a mix of both urban and rural areas. These local authorities face very different challenges in developing a thriving local micro market. Oldham, for example, had very few micro providers at the start of the project while Kent had a significant number of micro providers providing more traditional care services (eg. very small care homes).

The relevance of the project to all local authorities

Every local authority will have existing micro providers in their area but they can be hard to identify and engage; they face growing regulatory, legislative and other barriers and, in most areas, their numbers are falling. In every area there are entrepreneurs who would be willing and able to set up new, innovative and highly personalised service options if only they knew what people needed and had the information and support that they need to do so with confidence.

The NAAPS project is testing a business model that helps local authorities to work positively and creatively with current and potential micro providers and create an environment within which sustainable, safe and high quality micro services can thrive, providing real choice for people who need support and services. Our experience in the pilot areas of Oldham and Kent has helped us to understand what providers need and how best to help them. This learning is transferable to other areas providing the information and tools that local authorities need to support micro provision in their area.

Conclusions from phase 1 of the micro markets project

There has been a view that new services will simply emerge and thrive in response to the growing number of people with their own budgets. Evidence from the micro markets project suggests that this does not happen so easily.

Emerging providers

Learning from the project suggests that people who are interested in the idea of setting up a new service and who have the resources and skills necessary to deliver the service need intensive individualised help and support (hand holding) in order to make their idea a reality.

Existing providers

Providers of micro services are very well placed to take forward the government's strategy for self-directed support and are able to offer highly personalised services, tailored to the requirements of individuals. In order to do this they need information about the kinds of services that are required, and advice, help and support to transform their service where this is needed. Experience from current providers suggests that it can be extremely difficult for them to get clear and consistent guidance about the kinds of services that are now required and the changes that are needed from them. They struggle to engage and compete with larger providers and many are winding up their businesses or selling them to a bigger organisation.

Current micro providers have valuable skills and experience that are needed if we are to meet the requirements of everyone who needs support and services, however, they are increasingly leaving the sector.

The value of the agency support model

Evidence gained from the pilots suggests that the local support agency model can be very effective in stimulating and supporting the development of sustainable micro services.

In Oldham, over 19 months, the project:

- supported nine existing micro providers to become sustainable and deliver an effective and valued service
- supported the establishment of 15 sustainable new enterprises, providing services purchased by people with personal budgets
- supported a further 13 emerging providers who are not yet fully established.

In Kent, over 14 months, the project:

- worked with 41 established micro providers to help them understand the requirements of personalisation in Kent and transform their services to meet those requirements or manage the planned ending of their service
- supported the establishment of four new businesses in response to Kent's strategy for personalisation
- supported a further three emerging providers who are not yet fully established.

The essential features of successful agency support

Learning from the first phase of the pilot projects has helped us to identify the essential features of an agency that can successfully stimulate and support sustainable micro social care and support enterprises. These include:

- recognition by the local authority that work with micro enterprises is vital to shaping and building the market to ensure that choice is locally available
- understanding of the policy context of the work and in particular the clear links to Putting People First 2007
- the commitment of senior people in the local authority
- early engagement of people who have the power to drive forward the work
- proper resourcing
- a co-ordinator with the right attitude, approach and skills
- excellent working partnerships at all levels
- a clear remit and focus on outcomes for micro enterprises
- services that micro providers want and need
- barriers to micro enterprises are recognised, minimised or removed.

Phase 2: developing and testing a kitemarking approach for micro providers

The pilots have shown that the majority of emerging micro enterprises do not fall under any regulatory or legislative framework beyond the general common law duty of care (eg. leisure class designed to promote health and well-being; day support service that uses community facilities and public transport).

There is growing concern about the risk inherent in self-directed support and personal budgets. We need to guard against a one-size-fits-all approach to risk management and develop an approach for micro providers that is proportionate and appropriate. This second phase of the project will develop and test an approach to kitemarking and a quality assurance service that is tailored for micro social care enterprise. Learning from the development and testing of a kitemarking system for micro providers is expected to inform the approach to kitemarking taken for other types of unregulated provision and the approaches adopted by web-based information systems such as Care Bay and Shop4Support.

Experience from Hartlepool

Sarah Ward

Hartlepool is a north eastern coastal town with a population of 90,000. Up until 1996, Hartlepool was part of Cleveland County Council; once Cleveland disbanded, Hartlepool became a unitary authority.

Hartlepool have out-sourced the majority of their provision over the last 12 years resulting in there currently only being two in-house day services provided through the local authority and an intermediate care team, which works in the community, providing support and care in a short-term capacity to avoid premature admission to hospitals, residential care and also to allow speedy, safe discharge from hospital or residential settings.

On the whole, there is (I would say) quite a strong sense of community pride in Hartlepool and the local authority maintain four-star council status and a three-star adult social care rating. Over the last 10 years there have been extensive improvements to the town in relation to leisure and culture, resulting in a picturesque marina, housing developments, shops, restaurants and various leisure facilities such as a cinema, museum, and art gallery. Everything in Hartlepool in relation to facilities is fairly centralised making it more accessible to the community. The transport service is frequent and accessible in general terms. The distance from one side of Hartlepool to the other is approximately six miles.

There is a large voluntary sector network in Hartlepool (at the last count over 500 providers). An organisation called Hartlepool Voluntary Development Association (HVDA) co-ordinates the voluntary sector. It's a difficult task keeping up with the changes and updates around the provisions, and past attempts to log all the information on hard copy/disc has proved fairly ineffective due to the regular addition/ fall out of agencies or groups.

Hartlepool Borough Council are investing in a system called Hartlepool Now, which is a web-based information system, in an attempt to maximise citizens' access to up-to-date relevant information about what is available in their town and at what cost. The system should also provide ratings from other users regarding the quality and effectiveness of the service and a key part of the work will be to allocate the appropriate resource to keep the systems bang up-to-date.

Hartlepool and self-directed support

In March 2006 Hartlepool Borough Council made a decision to embark on the journey of transforming its adult social care system and signed up to receive support from the national In Control team, as their principles and values made sense to Hartlepool. In a matter of months Hartlepool expressed a wish to become one of the first 11 total transformation sites in the country making commitments to swift social care transformation. This brought many challenges and required commitments from every area of adult services and many extended areas of the council. There were many people within the council who didn't really see the need for the change and would argue that Hartlepool was a four-star council with a two-star (at the time) social services status. They would argue that we provide good reliable quality services to citizens of Hartlepool, and for the most part this was true.

Services at the time – including Extracare

The services that local authority and PCTs commissioned on behalf of users of health and social care support were limited. There was little choice in relation to providers, and the domiciliary (home care) services were contracted in relation to locality (ie. there were three mainstream care agencies each with a designated area that they were contracted to work in), resulting in social workers/care co-ordinators negotiating for people who needed support to go into a service with their area agency. This generally didn't do much to increase quality and flexibility and also stifled creativity – not only for individuals receiving social care but also for the workforce in exploring other options and resources. The department recognised a need to provide new and flexible ways of meeting individual needs and providing more choice. In relation to day opportunities there were:

- three older people's provisions
- a social skills centre for citizens with learning disabilities
- a centre for people of working age with a physical disability.

Overall, the older people's provision was difficult to sustain, as although the main centre was well used, fewer people were using them, making them less viable. The same applied to the centre for working age adults; the fact that people were starting to direct their own support through a direct payment was starting to have an impact on the usage of the building-based model of support. Prior to a system of personal budgets in Hartlepool, there was, as with many other local authorities across the country, a big push around the benefits/legal duty of direct payments, and as a result, people were commissioning their own support from a personal assistant or from a mainstream, universal type service such as their local gym, sports centre and general community facilities.

Something else that had an impact on Hartlepool and residential providers was the development of extra care across the town. This model provides people with differing levels of support needs regardless of how high or extensive their needs become. The largest of the extra care housing options in Hartlepool is a village type community with restaurants, shops, hairdressers, gym, pool, and 200 self-contained apartments or cottages. There is a doctor's surgery next door and the village is situated in a housing estate with plans for a park development close by. This model of support is not for everyone, and there are mixed views about whether the model creates inclusion or excludes people from their wider community. It is, however, another option for citizens of Hartlepool and many people who don't live in the village use the facilities on a regular basis. There are many people who were previously quite isolated who feel they now belong to a community.

The village's viability going forward relies on people who choose to live there opting for the support provided on-site. This automatically reduces choice and control in one sense and gives the provider the monopoly. However, the fact that support is available over 24 hours and is very flexible promotes people's independence and choice in the sense that they don't need to be supported to get up, or go to bed at a set time, for example, as the support is there throughout the day and night allowing flexibility.

Communicating the change: partnership with providers

The communication strategy in Hartlepool around self-directed support extended out to as many citizens/providers/workforce members as possible, outlining the scale of transformation we were hoping to achieve. There were regular events planned over time to elected members, citizens, the third sector, the whole workforce, community venues and facilities. Adverts were put in the local newspaper, the *Hartbeat* magazine, which is delivered to all homes within Hartlepool, and GP surgeries and clinics were given information. Generally, despite good communication, people's knowledge was still sketchy. However, providers started to understand the shift from local authorities and PCTs being their customers on a grand scale, to people becoming their customers and having much more choice and control resulting in less automatic assured work for them as agencies.

Potential new providers started to approach the department with different ideas and they wanted more information about how they should develop and what sort of support they should provide. The role of the local authority in this scenario was much more one of advice and support and it became clear that the individuals with personal budgets would be their customers – they needed to become an attractive choice for people. They needed to consider practical issues such as invoicing on an individual basis rather than on a whole block of hours invoiced to the local authority or PCT. Regular provider networks were set up.

From the onset of developing the systems of self-directed support in Hartlepool it has been evident that this system is much more transparent. In order to develop a working RAS (resource allocation system) there is a need to be explicit about costs of services and support in the current systems. Trying to gather information around the current costs was not an easy task, but was an invaluable exercise, not only as it enabled us to have a robust working RAS in the longer term, but it also highlighted the inconsistencies of some of the costs of support in relation to needs.

One example was where an individual had three separate hourly rates imposed on them by the same agency. Another example is three people living together in a supported living scenario, all with very different support needs receiving the same block purchased amount of support, with those less in need of support lending their funding to those with a much higher support need. This was obviously not sustainable in the long term and didn't promote the need for people to be seen as individuals who have different choices around how they receive their support. The cost for residential support reflects the national pattern of being much higher in 'specialist learning disability' type provision than in older people's provision. Prior to embarking on a system of self-directed support, there was much less emphasis on correlation between quality of support and cost. The question of would there be anything else the individual could do with the resource to get a better outcome was generally considered in the confines of what was available on the pick list of options that social workers were supplied with by the contract teams.

The fact that Hartlepool wanted to embrace 'total transformation' in a sense lessened the risk to forward thinking potential providers who previously couldn't scale up to the type of specifications that the local authority would put out to tender. The fact that a high number of people would have access to their social care monies created an opportunity for a natural development of new support in the local community. Existing contracted in-house providers very quickly started to think about the potential impact for them and some who had previously provided residential support started to consider if they could become more flexible in their approach and provide outreach type services.

A few years ago any young person requiring short break/respite type support would access in-house residential respite care or shared care situations. Often on reaching adulthood a young person would automatically transfer from the in-house residential respite option to the adults equivalent of which the local authority block purchased a number of beds at a set cost.

Because the beds were pre-set/paid for, there was a motivation to fill them. Indirectly, this led to individuals using respite over the level of their assessed need. It is understandable that if something has been paid for, social workers will strive to

ensure it is used to the maximum – not always mindful of the long-term dependency this may create.

Throughout the last 10 years, this culture has been created resulting in some people going through a transition from young people's/children's services to adult services, almost automatically receiving the equivalent blocks of day services support in replacement of school (five days from 9am–5pm) and blocks of respite type support in a building-based provision, without question or adequate exploration of other options.

Self-directed support creating a shift

With the onset of self-directed support in Hartlepool there has been a shift from the automatic use of building-based respite to the exploration of more individualised responses to adults having a short break and carers receiving a break from their 'caring/support' responsibilities.

Although children's services have not yet signed up to personal budgets, there are more innovative options being explored through direct payments. Adults' social workers in the field of transition are outlining the alternatives to building-based respite early on at the child's review in an attempt to break the cycle of automatic use of building-based day services and respite options, and reactive planning at the last minute often resulting in less choice and control.

This has led to many young adults having very different experiences and expectations. For example, some people are using their budgets to access mainstream leisure and community facilities, and paying family members or friends to support them in their activities. Some purchase a caravan and pay site fees through collective budgets, using informal family support networks. For example, two brothers go together with mother to the caravan, giving dad a break, or one brother goes with mother to give the other brother time with dad and vice versa. Sometimes both brothers may go with their sister. This works much better for the family than the two weeks respite a year the young men used to have at a holiday type respite provision, and was an extremely low cost option over time.

One person who previously had to spend a week every now and then in an older persons' respite residential setting uses a small budget of £1,500 a year to take regular breaks at a family run bed and breakfast in a nearby seaside town. As a result, this person has not been admitted to hospital for two years. Due to having full control of the money, she was able to avoid crisis by accessing a break when she felt that her mental health was deteriorating, rather than having to have a crisis intervention.

HUDSA (Hartlepool United Disabled Supporters Association) has allowed people with disabilities to access a more holiday type approach to respite/short breaks, which has also enhanced carers' respite. If a carer needs to have a holiday, the person they care for can also have a holiday independently of their parent/carer using either informal or paid support.

The new or alternative options that have developed around short break support have resulted in the local authority needing to review the number of block contracted beds in building-based residential support for people with learning difficulties. The number of older people taking up alternative respite/short breaks is also increasing, with many choosing options such as holiday type short breaks rather than building-based respite. However, there is also a move away from traditional day care models to individuals commissioning their own support. Some people have employed staff on an individual basis, in order to access more mainstream activities in their community. Some choose to purchase support through new agencies that do not have contracts with the Department. For example, agencies such as:

- CASS – Community Activity Sitting Service
- Your Time – agency
- Emergency Respite Care Scheme is a new scheme that provides up to 72 hours of emergency respite cover to carers where needed.

CASS

CASS provides blocks of support and a variety of activities that enable people to maintain social pursuits. The service has been created to provide a choice of services and support to meet the needs of people affected by dementia. The CASS service also provides a monthly Memory Lane Café where couples affected by dementia can enjoy social activities together with support at hand. The agency also provides information packs, advice and practical/emotional support to carers.

Your Time

Another agency, Your Time, provides support through blocks of support in people's homes to overnight support and this can also be purchased through a direct payment.

A group of people who formerly used building-based day services have sought business advice and used their direct payments/personal budgets to fund alternative accommodation, support and facilities/equipment to set up a drama group. Similarly, a media/film production group in Hartlepool, called Shoot Your Mouth Off (SYMO), have set up using the same model. Both of these groups have local acclaim and the people who use these provisions are very proud of their achievements (see the Department of Health DVD 'Increasing the uptake of Direct Payments').

Personalisation: Practical thoughts and ideas from people making it happen   © OLM-Pavilion 2009

Pathways to Independence

Pathways to Independence is another new provider that provides support to adults who have a disability. A number of people use their personal budgets to access individual or group support as an alternative to day services.

There is a piece of work being completed in the department to decommission block contracts and ensure individuals living in supported living/residential care have access to the information, benefits/money that they are entitled to. This has led to providers changing their approach and considering personalised responses as well as improving quality of life for individuals.

The last year and a half has highlighted to us that when people have more choice and control and have access to the money and the way it is used, they often choose very everyday type solutions to their support needs – often accessing mainstream options, thus supporting their local economy and diversifying the community. There are also natural developments that occur regarding alternatives to large-scale providers commissioned by the local authority/PCT.

The next step for Hartlepool is to focus much more on maximising universal services and social capital, as well as strengthening and developing inclusive communities in line with the Putting People First agenda. One thing is for sure – give people more control and things will start to happen and develop.

Chapter 5

Rosemary's story

Rosemary Berks

My name is Rosemary. I am a mum, wife and a grandma to the most beautiful little girl, Marissa.

I love my life! I want to share with you just a wee bit about how I live my life, in the philosophy of the social model of disability and as a citizen leader, both of which I am passionate about. I think it is important at this point to make the distinction between **impairment** and **disability**, within the social model approach.

So here goes.

I have been blind in my right eye since birth. I contracted polio when I was three. As a result, I was paralysed from the neck down, was in an iron lung for a time, in hospital for about a year, and had to learn to walk again.

About 15 years ago my mobility started to decrease. I have post polio syndrome, which means that I experience extreme fatigue and that all of the muscles that were affected by polio will weaken, which may result in paralysis again.

No one knows how long this process might take, so, on the bright side, I may die of old age, or get run over by a bus first!

I also have a cognitive impairment, or as I call it – 'my butterfly mind'. This means I find it difficult to concentrate, recall information, particularly sequential, so I need to read things over and over again to make sense of, or retain information.

So all of those things are my **impairments**.

My **disability**, however, is the disabling world that we all live in. This includes the physical, financial and attitudinal barriers that I and other disabled people face on a

daily basis. The biggest challenges by far are attitudinal barriers – sometimes blatant discrimination – often by well meaning people, who would never mean to offend and probably don't even know that they have been offensive. For example, the attitudes of people 50 years ago; when they said to my mum that I would have no quality of life they told her to have another healthy child to compensate for the fact that I would never be normal.

So, what is normal? This is normal for me. Your experience is normal for you, and so on for everyone.

So, being a normal child I wanted to go to school with my friends. But when it was time for me to go to school I faced attitudinal barriers in education too. People said it would be best for everyone if I attended the special school as I was a special child – my first label. There, I would be looked after and learn crafts and make things. They felt it would be a real problem for me to go to a mainstream school. Thankfully, my wee mummy realised that 'special' meant segregated and she challenged that decision. I attended primary school where, I admit, I was a problem, as I was always getting stuck climbing up the wall bars in the gym and sliding down the wooden banisters with my calliper on. Yes, I certainly was a 'problem', just not the kind of problem they had anticipated.

I went on to pass my 11+, attended high school, left there when I was 15, started work as an office junior and so on. I had the usual teenage trials, tribulations and romances. I met my first husband when I was 17 and was engaged at 18.

Some very well meaning people said that it was really good that I had a tall handsome fit young man to look after me and do things for me. Just before my 20th birthday we went to see our local vicar to arrange our wedding. He asked me if I could consummate the marriage and have children, which was a bit ironic, as I was about four months pregnant at the time.

I think I actually astounded some people by having not one, but two fabulous children.

I decided to leave my husband when I was 27 and was happily divorced soon after. For about three years I did all of the things I should have done when I was 17, vowing never to marry again.

Then I met my current husband, Graham. Within six months we had bought a house in Darlington, where Graham already lived, and moved there from Scotland, with my, now our, two children. One of the few things that Graham and I have in common is that we both love to travel. We've backpacked all over the world. Yes, my backpack was little and Graham's wasn't but it was still backpacking!

It was while we were travelling that I began to see the decrease in my mobility. As this progressed, I felt I needed the support of social services, who then came to visit me at home.

I was assessed by the care manager as needing a kettle tipper and a perch stool. The care manager couldn't get out of the door quick enough when I got upset. But I was grateful, of course.

When my mobility decreased yet again about three years ago, I was feeling really low, so I thought I'd give social services another go. We now lived in another area so I contacted the local council, where apparently I am a customer – another label.

My new care manager seemed to understand, I shared with her some very personal feelings, including about my relationship and the sadness I felt when I could not even hold my little granddaughter. I wasn't able to take her to nursery or to the park. This was so hard for me and my family.

My care manager also recognised that not being able to maintain my personal care, or keep my house the way I wanted it were major issues for me. I was exhausted all of the time and not able to cope any longer. She also understood that I did not want my husband to be my carer. I wanted him to be my husband! There is a difference.

My care manager was brilliant and took all of this to her line manager, who in her wisdom decided that I should only get four-and-a-half hours of direct payments support a week.

I was to have one hour of shopping once a week, a care agency that the council used to assist me with the housework twice a week, and the rest to be used for any medical appointments. I felt sorry for the care manager who had to tell me this. I felt that we both had gone through all of this for virtually nothing. I didn't have the energy to challenge the decision but I was grateful, of course.

When it came to my review, yet another care manager came. I was determined to be strong this time and I asked for more time than just an hour a week for shopping, as it takes 20 minutes just to get into town. I also asked for more flexibility and maybe some support to shop occasionally for clothes. I was told that the department would not provide support for disabled people to shop for clothes as this was not seen as being essential. She then said maybe there could be an exception at Christmas perhaps.

At the end of this session, which just got worse, I had honestly felt worthless. She asked if I would be okay. We both knew what she was saying. I reassured her by telling

her that I used to be the director of Darlington Samaritans so I knew the number. She said 'oh good', looked relieved and left.

My support went up to seven-and-a-half hours per week and I was grateful, of course.

The standards of the care agency, which was allocated to assist me with housework, were just awful. It made me more and more depressed. I felt I couldn't challenge this in case I ended up without any support. I had to go over everything with all of the different people who came into my home wearing their carer's uniform.

There was no confidentiality or professional boundaries as they all talked about the other individuals who they worked for. I tried to be polite and change the subject and as someone who values their privacy but lives in a little village, I wondered what they were saying about me. All of this caused more tension in my relationship and things just got worse. The care agency and I finally parted company but not before one of the 'care workers' said, in the middle of my housework, *'I'm just nipping out to put Mavis on the toilet, I'll be back soon'*. The worst thing being that I just couldn't say anything, so that's exactly what she did, on more than one occasion.

I did move on from this, with the support of my own organisation and my family. I did my own kind of 'support plan' and I discovered that under the fair access to care services (FACS) criteria that I am 'critical' – another label. After what felt like torture and a battle of wills, I was allocated 27.5 hours per week – still as a direct payment. With these hours, although still not with the flexibility a personal or individual budget hopefully will bring, I have been able to get the life I want.

This has made such a difference. I now use the services of a highly professional eco-friendly cleaning company who come when I want them to and do what has been agreed in a joint contract. I also now employ three personal assistants. The result of all of this is that I have been really well (apart from the dreaded flu, which I suppose is equality!).

This means I've had hardly any time off work and have not used all of my direct payment hours. I feel OK and I have some choices. The most positive impact this has had is about how I feel about myself, my self-esteem, both in my personal and professional life, where I also receive access to work.

My work is really important to me. I work for Darlington Association On Disability and we work in partnership with our local authority. For example, we deliver disability equality training to all of their staff, we advise on impact assessments and we have interviewed and recruited key staff to the personalisation team. We are able to influence and affect

positive change, campaigning for and promoting equality and, of course, the social model of disability. The support I get from Access to Work has made this possible.

I have taken on the role of citizen leader (a label that I am proud of) and I feel confident in this role. It was in this role that I contacted the local lead on personalisation. He seemed quite keen to involve disabled people, so when I suggested that if this were to be effective, and people were valued, did they actually pay for peoples' time and expertise? His reply was that in his experience, *'Disabled people were quite happy to come along to a meeting, get their transport paid for, have a sandwich/lunch and a nice card at Christmas!'* I've also heard from senior managers, *'Well, we have to get this right you know, one day we may be old, or disabled'*.

This is a classic example of well meaning people who don't see this as an equality issue. There is a long way to go, but I'm still optimistic.

So I'd like to finish with some key thoughts.

- I don't want to be labelled, unless I choose that label.
- I don't want to be told that I can get support to go to the toilet etc. once, twice or three times a day.
- A very wise woman said, if you ask a question in a prescriptive way, you will get the response in a prescriptive way and therefore measure in a prescriptive. I think we need to remember this.
- I don't need help, which reinforces the professional gift model. I need support.
- If I tell you about my access needs and you need clarification then that's OK. If my access needs are continually not met then when does a physical barrier turn into an attitudinal barrier?
- I don't want to have to feel grateful anymore.
- I don't want to be special, I just want to be an equal citizen.
- I want to live my life within the social model of disability.
- I don't want people making decisions about me based on their professional expertise.
- I am the expert, on my life, based on my experience.

Chapter 6

Personalised support

Doreen Kelly

Partners for Inclusion exists to:

- support people with disabilities to live how they choose, while influencing and enhancing the opportunities available to all
- share knowledge, experiences and learning with others.

Partners for Inclusion believes:

- everyone is equal and different, with their own gifts
- everyone has the ability to develop
- everyone has needs and the right to support in keeping with their basic human rights
- everyone's relationships are valuable.

Partners for Inclusion provides tailored services to people with learning and/or mental health difficulties. Each service is unique, created from bespoke planning and designed to meet the needs of the person being supported. Partners for Inclusion supports people who have left long-stay institutions and moved into their own home, and some people who live with their parents and may wish to move out if and when the time is right. For those who have their own home, it is indeed their own home. The person has their own tenancy or mortgage and thus their own security. Tenure is not linked to support. Furthermore, each person has their own support team, comprising of staff matched to their own likes and dislikes. The staff member who is right to support one person may not be right for another. Partners for Inclusion's aim is to support people to have real lives, with jobs, friends and relationships. That means that each and every person is successfully supported, regardless of their perceived complexity of need. Partners for Inclusion has a reputation for supporting people who have traditionally been viewed as 'challenging' to get the life that is right for them – supporting those people who have been the most excluded to 'belong'.

Partners for Inclusion grew out of Inclusion Glasgow, another small organisation, set up by Simon Duffy, based on the same principles, and along with C-Change for Inclusion, support each other to promote this particular way of working. Partners supports only 45 people and will not support more. This is a further component of the design. Partners wishes to value and work with the people it already supports, not to always have its energy focused on growth. The organisation will, however, support the growth of a new, autonomous project in order to respond to the need for person-centred services. This new project is called Just Connections.

Partners for Inclusion attracts labels like 'creative' and 'inspired', but what is the method? Like all supported living services, Partners is bound by compliance with legislation and regulation. Its main funding local authorities are no less stringent than anywhere else, and its staff, while wonderful, are not capable of magic. The magic is in the method, the understanding of the 'how'.

The 'how'

The organisation

Hierarchy within Partners for Inclusion is as flat as possible. Governance comes from a voluntary board comprising of parents of the people who the organisation supports, a lawyer, senior manager from another similar organisation, and financial and business consultants. The board are 'hands off' from the strategic and operational running of the organisation. This is headed up by the director and deputy director and the finance director. Service leaders are each responsible for the operations within several supported living services and each service has its own staff team, most with its own team leader. (One team is currently self-directed because that's what works for them). Over and above, there is a small finance team, training team and admin team. The central management team is office based and discreet from the 45 services. People's lives do not operate from the central office. There is also an employment development co-ordinator whose role it is to support each person and their team in the search for meaningful employment.

Designing a service

Partners for Inclusion receives most referrals from social work, who will initially get in touch to ask if a service can be provided for a particular person. However, there are no exclusions to how people can be introduced to the organisation including self-referral, family contact and referrals from other professionals. So begins the planning, or 'start up' period. Partners for Inclusion cannot provide a service overnight but experience tells us that a period in the region of three months is necessary to get to know the person and those people important to the person in order to design the service and then put it in place. An early step though, would be for the director or another senior

member of staff to introduce themselves to the person and their family and check out if they wish Partners to provide the service.

Step 1: funding

Partners for Inclusion looks forward to when individual budgets and In Control is commonplace in Scotland. In the meantime, Partners continues to get most of its funding from local authorities and sometimes as a block contract, however, the money for all people supported is treated internally as if it were an individual budget. A manager or one of the directors will meet with the funders to discuss the referral and agree costs and budgets. People may be funded directly by the local authority or through a combination of local authority monies, independent living fund, direct payments or ideally in the future individual budgets. Each person who Partners for Inclusion supports has an 'individual service fund', which means the money the funder pays is individually ring-fenced to them. Central costs are taken off for admin, training, service leader etc. but the main body of the money is used exclusively for that person's service; the money therefore is viewed as being the person's not the organisation's. This is managed via quarterly budget meetings, which look at how the year's money is doing and plan for any up and coming costs. These meetings are attended by the person receiving the service, if they wish to come along, their staff team, family members and the service leader. Everyone sits down with the finance director or a member of the finance team and plans together. The money is not managed from a distance but is right there and transparent to all involved.

Step 2: planning

The purpose of the planning days is to create a unique service design and working policy for that person; it is this that makes the person's service bespoke. The service design is the big picture of **what** the person's service will look like, and the working policy is the detail of **how** to implement the service.

The right service leader will be selected from the central team and he or she will meet with the person and their family and arrange a 'planning day'. This will happen even if there is an existing care plan, person-centred plan or essential lifestyle plan, or other professional assessment, in place. While these documents will be used, Partners for Inclusion believes that direct planning with the person cannot be substituted. The planning is about how to turn a person-centred plan into how Partners will design and deliver the person's service. The service leader will ask the person and their family who they would like to come along to this day, the first step in the process of designing the service.

Partners for Inclusion knows that for some people who have lived in institutions for a long time, they have sometimes lost touch with their family. In this case, it may be

staff who come along, maybe someone's key worker or advocate, or it may be the tea lady who has served tea for the last 20 years and has a special relationship with the person. This day is built around the person and this is the case regardless of any 'labels' the person may have been assigned. Partners for Inclusion will work very hard to find out who the right people are to come along if the person cannot use words to tell us themselves. This means the service leader spending time with the person to work some of this out. The service leader will also work with the person to establish how the day should be organised. For example, where should it be held? How long should sessions run for? Should there be music, photographs? What should be served for lunch? How should the day start and finish? Does drama work for the person? Should it involve swimming? Should everyone go for a long walk? Basically, Partners will ensure that this day is meaningful to the person and 'floats their boat' more than anyone else's. Our experience is that it is very difficult to get people to come to traditional meetings; this is often because people have had negative experiences of meetings in the past.

The day is normally facilitated by one of the directors and the service leader. Big bits of paper are put on the wall and all the information is recorded in words and graphics. The group will set ground rules before starting and the facilitators will assist the group in sticking with them.

The planning day itself will start at the beginning and ask the person and those with the person to tell their story. We ask the person to tell us what has happened in their life so far. Time is spent listening to the highs and lows, and this is recorded on the paper on the wall. Often this can be an emotional experience for the person and those close to them. If a second day is needed this will be arranged. Hearing the person's story helps to begin seeing a real person as opposed to anything else. Highs will be celebrated and lows heard and respected. The words used by the person and those around them will be the words recorded. The story will offer lots of clues about who the person is and what works or not for them. By doing this, the evidence starts to build about what kind of service would suit the person well. The best predictor of the future is often the past.

Following this, the process will move on to looking at how the person's service is to be designed. Partners for Inclusion uses a range of person-centred planning tools to assist with this process. These include, MAP and PATH and essential lifestyle planning. The key to getting the right design is detail and avoidance of generalisations and assumptions.

Partners for Inclusion will seek to find out from the people at the planning day as much detail as possible about how the service should look and feel. Partners for Inclusion has designed a framework to ensure all areas are covered. Partners for Inclusion will ask the following questions.

- What are the person's essentials, likes and dislikes, hopes and dreams and nightmares?
- What are the person's hobbies, interests, gifts and talents?
- Who are the people who love and care about the person? What do we need to do to help make sure important family bonds and friendships are maintained?
- How do the people who love and care about the person describe him or her?
- What are the person's routines?
- How will the person get out and about on a daily basis?
- What does the person want to do with their life, for example, education or work?
- What would make the ideal house for the person?

This should be asked even if a house has already been chosen for the person, as it's such an important part of getting the service right. A good way to get this information is to start by thinking about who the person is, what their hopes and dreams are, and what relationships are important to them, and to then think about where the house might be – in the country, a village, town or city. The next question is, bearing in mind what the person likes to do with their time, what would they need available in the community, or in their street, and so on, bringing it in until decisions have been made about the size of house, type of house, and what furniture and fixtures need to be in the house. There may be physical needs etc.

Getting the right house is a fundamental component of getting the service right. If the house doesn't match the person it's unlikely to work as the following example illustrates.

Paul left long-stay hospital and moved into his own flat in a quiet cul-de-sac, which was on the ground floor in a block of four. Paul is noisy a lot of time, always has been and most likely always will be. That is who he is. This soon became a problem for him and for his neighbours. The majority of his neighbours were elderly and found the noise difficult to cope with. Eventually they raised a petition for his eviction and the local authority began considering if Paul needed to live in a group home or secure accommodation. Paul hadn't changed, yet he found himself in a vulnerable situation because the house wasn't right from the outset. Partners worked hard to find alternative accommodation for Paul but couldn't find anything suitable within public housing stock. The net was cast wider into the private sector and eventually a farmhouse was found with no neighbours but close enough to town to not be completely isolated. The rent was higher for this property than for local authority housing, however, close working with the housing benefit office resulted in his full rent being paid by housing benefit. Paul has lived there quite happily now for two years.

■ How does the person communicate?

What is the right staff team for the person? What attributes should staff have and not have? What will the roles of the staff be? How should interviews take place and new staff be introduced? How many staff hours are required to properly cover the service and allow for annual leave and training? Getting this calculation right means that the team can cover all the hours and the person will not have people he or she doesn't know supporting them. A good way to find out what makes an ideal staff member is to establish who has worked well in the past with the person and then break down their qualities and detail why that worked well, and then who did not work well with the person. This allows for a picture to be built of what should be worked towards and what should be avoided. The formation of the staff team also needs to be considered with gender balance, different experiences and skills etc.

■ What will the service look like – hours of support, sleepovers?
■ How should we support the person to keep healthy and safe – physical and mental health, medication, moving and handling, healthy eating, input from health professionals?
■ Does the person need support with personal care? How should this happen?
■ What training do staff need to provide support?
■ How do we support the person to look after their new home and manage their money?
■ What are the overall aims and objectives of the service?

This list is not exhaustive and the framework is only a guide to be added to, however, all of the above points are important. There is no right or wrong answer to any of the above and the facilitators will spend time fully exploring each area, encouraging the person and those others to fully explore and define each answer.

This is then written into the service design by the service leader and becomes the blueprint for that person's unique service. Once this information is gathered, the service leader can begin recruiting staff based on information gathered on the planning day(s). This recruitment process differs for each person Partners supports, as everyone's service is different. However, there are a few key principles that are always followed.

■ Staff must be 'matched' to the person as defined in the service design. Each person supported has their way of employing staff – this should be detailed in the person's service design.
■ Managers are not empowered to make final recruitment decisions; the person receiving the support makes the final decision about whether or not to employ the applicant.

Personalisation: Practical thoughts and ideas from people making it happen   © OLM-Pavilion 2009

Sometimes the person will be involved in all the interviews and sometimes the service leader will do initial interviews and if someone is felt to be a 'match' arrange for them to meet the person for a coffee or a walk. Sometimes the potential employee will be asked to meet the person two or three times before everyone feels ready to make a decision. Sometimes family and friends will be involved. However, what is fundamental is that the person themselves, or where this is not possible, their family, friend or representative makes the final decision, letting us know if they wish to be supported by this person.

Step 3: the detail

Having undertaken the initial planning and begun the recruitment process, the service leader will go on to arrange a 'working policy' day. The 'working policy' like the service design is unique to the person and the service. It is the fine detail of how Partners for Inclusion will support the person, covering all aspects of the person's life. No detail is too fine and this document will include how staff will respond when the person is finding life difficult and feeling anxious or upset, where to stand, what to say, who to call etc. It will also detail how the person prefers to be worked with such as preferences around how personal care is carried out, how the person gets up, goes to bed, enjoys meals and so on. Again, all the important people in the person's life will be included in this session (or sessions), although sometimes the person and their family may choose not to be included as often this can feel negative as it is necessary here to talk about the difficulties from the past in order to learn what worked and didn't work to get things right in the future. The appropriate professionals and others that work with the person need to be included as this is where all the necessary people sign up to the detail of how the support will be provided. The working policy, which could otherwise be described as staff guidance, becomes the rules of how the staff team will respond in any given situation. It must be tight, specific and detailed. The working policy acts as a measure and is used to compare what happened when things go wrong with what should have happened, therefore, it is a useful tool for all.

An example of what it would not say is: *'When Joe gets upset he should be encouraged to return home.'*

An example of what it might say is:

> *'Sometimes when Joe is out he may become anxious. He lets us know this by shaking his head and counting on his fingers. If Joe does this, staff should say to Joe, "OK Joe, I can see you're not happy, let's walk back to the car and go home". This lets Joe know you understand how he's feeling. Staff should go on and prompt Joe to gather his belongings by saying "OK Joe, get your things".*

When Joe has got his things staff should walk alongside him to return to the car. Joe should always walk on the inside. On reaching the car, staff should open the passenger door and say to Joe "OK Joe, you get in the car now" and let Joe get in the car. Joe will step into the car himself and normally put his seatbelt on (detail of how Joe travels in his car will be detailed in another section). If Joe does not put his seatbelt on staff should prompt him by saying "OK Joe, can you put your seat belt on?" Our experience is that Joe will always do this. In the event Joe will not put his seatbelt on, staff should say to Joe, "OK Joe I'm going to wait outside the car until you are ready to put your belt on and then we'll go." Staff should then close the car door and wait close by on the pavement.'

This is only one example but shows the detail the working policy will contain and highlights the importance of everyone signing up to it. Everyone should be clear and in agreement about how staff are going to respond. It is by doing the detailed work around past incidents that make it possible to come up with a response that is most likely to work if and when incidents occur in the future. The best and possibly only predictor for the future is the past.

Partners for Inclusion takes a very responsible approach to managing risk but is not risk averse. For people to be supported to build real and meaningful lives for themselves risk is inherent. The working policy and Partners for Inclusion's common sense health and safety processes work out how to do this in a safe manner without intruding on the person's choices and quality of life. The health and safety processes are about how to do things safely – they are not about stopping people from doing things and living their lives.

Step 4: pulling it all together

Once recruited, staff will undertake their mandatory training. This means the core training required to be a part of a person's service. Every new staff member has an induction, learning about the core values of the organisation, first aid, food hygiene, health and safety and general moving and handling. There is then the individually tailored training, which may include epilepsy, autism and CALM (crisis and aggression limitation management). Within CALM and epilepsy training, staff are only trained in what they will need. For example, if the person they will go on to support has epilepsy but is not written up for any rescue medication, the staff will undertake epilepsy awareness but not be trained in the administration of rectal diazepam or midazolam. Similarly, each person supported by Partners for Inclusion receives a CALM assessment, which establishes which techniques the staff require to support each person. Staff are then only trained in those techniques. Those techniques are verified externally and staff practise these at team meetings and are refreshed and reverified annually. Any use of CALM within the organisation results in a reporting and review process to ensure learning is captured.

Partners for Inclusion works hard to equip its staff with the skills and knowledge they need to do their work well but does not believe in 'one size fits all' even for training.

New staff begin working with the person on a shadowing basis. That is working alongside either the person's family or existing staff to observe how things are done. This will move from observation to taking the lead at a pace that is right for the person and the staff and so the team and the service begins to take shape.

As the new team get to know the person and vice versa, the service design and working policy will be updated to include the new learning and understanding. During this period, Partners staff will go from spending short periods of time with the person to gradually spending more time with the person. Where a service is new the person will most likely be getting their house ready, involving lots of shopping and organising and the new staff team will support the person with this and getting to know their new local community and what happens there.

The team will have lots of meetings and spend time team building and working out how they will work as a team. This will be led by the service leader and team leader and set the tone for future working. All teams have team building or team development days at least once a year to keep them focused and fresh.

The service leader will also spend time liaising with the professionals involved in the person's support and working out how the wider support team of professionals, where applicable, will fit into the service. This is another crucial element to getting it right. If the work is done to establish relationships in this area, it will be easier to plan when things are tough.

Step 5: money matters

The service leader will work out if the person needs support with their money. Support can range from Partners for Inclusion being fully involved in supporting the person with their money, to the person having their own account set up under the Partners for Inclusion umbrella and only requiring minimal support, or the person may need no input at all around managing their money in which case they will have their own arrangements. Where involvement is required this means that while the account is set up and maintained by Partners for Inclusion, the person has their own individual named current account, based at their local branch. Again, this keeps things person-centred and ensures the person's money is as close to them as possible. If full financial support is required, the support team would then work within the remit of the Partners for Inclusion finance policy to manage the person's money, with the person's benefits and/or income being paid into this account.

Another account will be set up for staff support expenses. The organisation will put a set amount in this account each week and the team will be delegated responsibility in keeping with the finance policy, to manage this money for the benefit of supporting the person to get out and about and get a life. The amount for this will be agreed at initial budget meetings. This money is to cover travel and other expenses needed as part of supporting the person. For example, if the person and their support worker go out for tea, the person will pay for their own meal and staff will pay for theirs from the support account.

Full audits are carried out twice yearly and secure procedures are in place to guard against fraud, however, these procedures take place in the background and are discreet.

Step 6: and go!

The start up period will normally last a minimum of three months but sometimes can be longer. When everyone is ready Partners for Inclusion will begin supporting the person.

For Partners for Inclusion this is where the real work starts. Supporting the person to get this elusive real life for themselves – find that job, make those friends. The very individual set up of each service means that change can happen easily and the service can evolve as the person does. This may mean extra support through tough times but equally less support when the person is ready to spread their wings. It means unconditional support, through thick and thin and all life's up and downs. Partners for Inclusion always believes there's a way and will always seek to find it. Partners have never found themselves in a position where they are saying someone is too difficult or not possible to support. Due to flexibility of how the service is set up, all elements of the service can change if it is not working for the person. The staff can change; where the person lives or who they live with can change; the person's routines and what they do with their time can change, allowing the organisation over the years to support people regardless of the challenges involved. While the organisation will never say they cannot support a person, it is respected and encouraged if the person receiving support wants to change who provides the support.

Planning days are held annually to review what's happened in the past year and plan for the next year and service designs are updated on the back of this. This allows time to pause, consider and reflect and ensures Partners for Inclusion are continually striving to provide the right service. Working polices are continually evolving as the person themselves evolves. This document is always a work in progress and is kept up-to-date.

Keeping to this simple blueprint ensures that Partners for Inclusion continues to provide individual person-centred services that suit people really well.

Chapter 7

Risk and safeguarding
Risk

Viv Slater

> 'Security is mostly a superstition. It does not exist in nature, nor do the children
> of men as a whole experience it. Avoiding danger is no safer in the long run than
> outright exposure. Life is either a daring adventure or nothing.'
>
> Helen Keller

This chapter will explore issues of risk in a new personalised world, and look particularly at two working practices that can help – supported decision-making and risk enablement processes.

Personalisation is grounded in principles that include citizenship, human rights, the social model of disability, and the right of all people. This includes those people who need social care support to get on with their lives, to self-determine how they live their lives, what risks they choose to take, and what counts as a good decision about how to navigate the inevitable challenges.

It is vital that we remember that in moving to a personalised way of operating social care, we are not moving from a risk free environment in the current system, or even a stable and satisfactory position to one full of risks. If we think that we are ignoring the evidence in front of our eyes in relation to what happens to people in institutions whether they are old or young – what can happen when people are supported in a non-personalised way, whether in their own home or not? We should be concerned about the most vulnerable people in the 'system', for instance younger adults in care settings, often for long periods of their lives, and older people with dementia, sometimes in care placements where countless inspections and reports have highlighted the dangers to them of isolation, administration of drugs that are detrimental to health, and difficulty in getting direct contact with primary health services.

So we are not moving from a risk free environment – but neither are we moving towards a personalised world free of risks. There are plenty – and because they are often different in nature to the ones we have grown accustomed to, they can appear more challenging.

However, we must hold on to the key reasons that underpin personalisation (those principles above) and demand that the new system delivers better opportunities for disabled adults and older people.

When considering a move towards a process of self-directed support, it is important to remember that by initially identifying a fair and reasonable 'indicative' amount for a person to use to meet the outcomes of their choice, that we are not just giving away an amount of money to discharge statutory duties. The support plan must still be signed and approved by the social worker (or in some circumstances team manager) on behalf of the local authority to highlight how all identified needs/outcomes have been considered and the plan will indeed support the person to remain healthy, safe and well.

Duffy and Gillespie (2009) in their paper, *Personalisation and Safeguarding* drafted for In Control suggest that:

'By shifting the role of the local authority towards that of interrogator, checker and approver (of the plan) it encourages a creative dialogue that radically reduces the risk of ill considered plans and services.'

This shift enables people to organise their support and services in ways that make sense to them, exploring people's own solutions and enabling real choice and preference about who supports very specific needs. This allows social workers to have an overview and will sign off the support plan, exploring outcomes with the person, identifying possible areas that may need further exploration.

Independence, Well-being and Choice (Department of Health, 2005) asked the question, what was the right balance in managing risks, and people fed back that there was a need to address issues of risk aversion in practice. *Our Health, Our Care, Our Say* (Department of Health, 2006) made a commitment to develop a national approach to risk in social care. With increased choice, empowerment and control comes a need to address issues around rights, responsibility and risk.

Adopting a more positive, person-centred approach to risk encourages services to look for new ways to support and empower the people they work with. Taking this approach can involve people who need support, and their families, in decisions made about risk taking.

What is obviously clear is that people should not be supported to take unreasonable risks, nor should they be funded to do so – local authorities still have duties and responsibilities that mean they can legitimately withdraw involvement in situations they perceive to be too risky. However, they should be able to demonstrate why this is the case, and be open to challenge given the likelihood of a culture of risk aversion.

Avoiding risk altogether is not an option. This would constrain the choices people make, and still wears emperor's clothes in relation to our current system and some of the unacceptable risks it places people under.

The Department of Health's choice and risk framework (2007) identifies some principles to guide local authorities when considering risk.

- Help people understand their responsibilities and the implications of their choices, including any risks.
- Acknowledge that there will always be some element of risk, and that trying to remove it altogether can outweigh the quality of life benefits for the person.
- Never expose people to an unreasonable level of risk.
- Never forget the rights of people to self-determine and to choose which set of risks is preferable.

A good example of this last point of these principles is an elderly lady, who following a hip fracture, hospital stay, and a 'ready for discharge' decision by her consultant had a blunt choice to make – whether to accept the risks of a residential placement for the rest of her life or return to her home environment, which was messy, risky and the one in which she had suffered her recent fall. Given good understanding of the risks – the choice would have been something like:

A. Residential home – will be warm, fed, washed as a minimum but 20 miles away from home, friends can't visit, GP who she has known her for 35 years will no longer be her GP, loss of control over life, not in keeping with chosen lifestyle (private, self-determining, independent).
B. Return home – familiar environment, still in local network of friends and family, still seeing GP but untidy, risky physical environment that can't be fully mitigated by adaptations, some isolation that will contribute to risk, physical health means further falls likely, dislike of technology means that basic telecare (warden alarm) may not be used.

In this example the 'system' decided that it was too risky for her to return home; she was told that this was the case and accepted the decision, went to live in the residential home, quickly became depressed and died within six weeks, despite arriving at home in relatively good health. We cannot know the outcome if she had returned home, but those who know her best including her son and her neighbours know that her choice in relation to risk would clearly have been to go home, lessen risk as far as possible and live with the consequences. Living her last weeks away from her home with strangers in a place she did not want to be was her worst nightmare.

Practical pointers for local authorities in managing risk well were recommended in *Independence, Choice and Risk: A guide to supported decision-making* (Department of Health, 2007). A summary follows.

- A good approach to choice and risk is that people have the right to live their lives to the full as long as that does not stop others from doing the same.
- Fear of supporting people to take reasonable risks in their daily lives can prevent them from doing the things that most people take for granted.
- What needs to be considered is the consequence of an action and the likelihood of any harm from it.
- By taking account of the benefits in terms of independence, well-being and choice, it should be possible for a person to have a support plan that enables them to manage identified risks and to live their lives in ways that best suit them.
- The human rights of people must underpin the actions and decisions of all, irrespective of the setting.
- Resource pressures should not lead to placing individuals at risk.
- The most important resource is often time spent with the person to develop a good support plan.
- An individual approach should be taken for all adults.
- Use of a supported decision tool is recommended to record a discussion of the person's choices and any inherent risks.
- Carers' needs and wishes must be acknowledged, and any conflict of wishes must support the rights of all involved.

Supported decision-making

Independence, Choice and Risk (Department of Health, 2007) offers a supported decision-making tool that includes the following suggested checklist for consideration by local authorities when working with people. This information is best gathered through conversation with people.

- What is important to you in your life?
- What is working well?
- What isn't working so well?
- What could make it better?
- What things are difficult for you?

- Describe how they affect you living your life.
- What would make things better for you?
- What is stopping you from doing what you want to do?
- Do you think there are any risks?
- Could things be done in a different way, which might reduce the risks?
- Would you do things differently?
- Is the risk present wherever you live?
- What do you need to do?
- What do staff/organisation need to change?
- What could family/carers do?
- Who is important to you?
- What do people important to you think?
- Are there any differences of opinion between you and the people you said are important to you?
- What would help to resolve this?
- Who might be able to help?
- What could we do (practitioner) to support you?
- Agreed next steps – who will do what?

Another tool useful for supporting a different approach to risk, and a challenge to the existing culture of likely risk aversion in practice for local authorities is the process of risk enablement.

Risk enablement process

The self-directed support implementation team in Oldham, which adopted the process of risk enablement back in 2005, very often tried to explain the concept of this process as having the clue in the title – it is about risk 'enablement'.

Risk enablement process is a mechanism that a number of local authorities are now adopting to embed a new approach to risk, to ensure that the potential current risk aversion is tackled, to embed transparency in the process, and to create a culture of self-determination, within responsible and appropriate local authority practice.

Risk enablement will:

- recognise that the local authority still has a duty of care
- look at the risk in context; will the risk be present wherever the person lives
- creatively seek solutions that promote rights and choice
- share the decision-making process
- accurately record decisions taken.

As mentioned above, the best antidote to risk is a really good support plan that asks all the 'what if' questions and searches out the best answers that are still in keeping with the wishes and choices of people. Most systems require sign off of support plans, including the risks and how they are going to be mitigated. This should show evidence that the plan is reasonable, is the best way of supporting someone's life and their chosen outcomes, and enhancing the person's chances of being healthy, safe and well.

However, if it is considered that the plan does not, instead of the system imposing a different choice on people by refusing the support they want and only offering an alternative that is congenial to the local authority, the idea of a risk enablement process emerged. The panel approach ensures transparency about decision-making, makes possible the concept of co-production in relation to planning and risk, and can consider at least two of three options:

- plan agreed – original refusal rooted in current risk aversion – person has right to choose a particular set of risks over another
- plan modified and agreed – extra checks and balances put in place that are to everyone's satisfaction
- plan refused – risk too high.

The panel should have multidisciplinary membership to mitigate inappropriate influence from one profession and culture, should be transparent and open, and conducted in such a way that invites and supports involvement of people and families. Any party at any point needs to be able to refer to risk enablement for support around specific issues and conflict resolution, including care managers, providers, family members or individuals.

However, panels processes must not happen in isolation – they need to be embedded in cultural change strategies that are built on choice, empowerment and risk management policies that promote more open and transparent practices. They need to be visibly supported by senior leadership and shared across organisations. They need to ensure that no one party, including people and their families, carers, care managers or providers, is left managing the risks alone.

There are many advantages of developing a risk enablement process. The following strengths are some that were highlighted in the Department of Health's Personalisation Resource Toolkit: Developing a risk panel (more detailed information, including practical help on how to develop a risk panel, terms of reference, membership of group, skills and knowledge required for members of the group and other practicalities can be found on www.dhcarenetworks.org.uk/personalisation/PersonalisationToolkit).

The adoption of a risk enablement process as part of the local authority process can do the following:

- offer advice, guidance and consistency of approach and includes senior staff
- be holistic in its approach
- articulate a way in which the organisation shares the risk
- present a position that enables recognition of the wider picture of types of risk emerging and the risks to independence of 'not enabling or supporting choice'
- offer a 'sense of relief' through a supportive second opinion
- offer a position that is one step removed as it enables reflection on what is happening in a given situation, that makes 'sense' of the risk and thinks more widely (eg. a holistic view)
- provide an opportunity to resolve conflicting standpoints and make decisions
- supporting and/or challenge established staff thresholds of risks
- enable a focus on contingency planning in advance of crises
- contain differing levels of anxiety from different parties,

However, the biggest advantage of adopting this process into an organisation is that it shares responsibility and records a process for enabling risks – supporting the fundamental culture shift towards self-determination, which is required for people to be truly self-directive of their support.

There are a number of practical resources available and a step-by-step guide for developing a risk enablement process to be found on www.dhcarenetworks.org.uk/personalisation/PersonalisationToolkit. These guides are really helpful to develop the thinking and resources required for implementation.

It is essential that a fundamental culture shift for organisations and individuals will be absolutely crucial if we want to achieve the vision of self-determination for people who use any element of social care of the future. Our current system of regulation, accreditation and qualification enables professionals to be protected behind a fascia of apparent 'competence'. It is believed that if people maintain these processes and systems that safety will ensue. However, even in the current system it this is not delivered and people are still exposed (even more so those people who fund their own support).

Duffy and Gillespie (2009) in their paper for In Control, *Personalisation and Safeguarding*, explored the concept of citizen-based prevention, which argues that the current 'professional gift' system deprives people from building networks of natural support. Linking members of 'communities' (whichever definition of this we choose to take) and developing or building on real relationships with others could provide an individual structure/framework to help people to stay safer than some of the current

systems including regulation and accreditation. After all, relationships are the core of what makes us tick as human beings. If people are isolated and alone, should this too not be seen as a risk – to our 'humanness'? This is something that at present largely remains theory as it is early days for personalisation and currently only one per cent of people who use social care services do so via this route. However, as practitioners, if we can change the culture of 'risk' and prevention, and be able to explore risk for people on an individual basis, circumstances as we saw in the earlier example of the elderly lady who died following her removal from her home should become less frequent.

In summary, good practice for local authorities in managing risk should ensure they are able to illustrate, as priorities, how they:

■ establish the person's needs, wishes and lifestyle choices using any communication aids necessary
■ promote the use of advocacy or supported decisions to ensure the person's interests and rights are protected
■ always consider the person's choices, even where the risks cannot be totally eliminated
■ consider that the 'safest option' may not be necessarily the best option for the person and may be detrimental to quality of life and a risk to maintaining independence to a person.

Our Health, Our Care, Our Say (2006) laid the vision of *'fair and responsive health and social care that helped you to stay healthy, independent and well and would give the best possible care when you need help'*. In developing a new system of personalised support specifically around managing risk, we need to ensure one which empowers all people who need support to live their lives, to be able to make real choices and take real risks; and also to empower those who are responsible for the statutory duties, so that they are empowered to listen to people and enable real choice to deliver real control.

Risk in a personalised world has to be managed in very personalised ways. Risks will be different for all people and how to handle this in a personalised world is to develop the systems and processes to explore choice and control and rights vs. risk.

References

Department of Health (2005) *Independence, Well-being and Choice: Our vision for the future of social care for adults in England*. London: Department of Health.

Department of Health (2006) *Our Health, Our Care, Our Say*. London: Department of Health.

Department of Health (2007) *Independence, Choice and Risk: A guide to supported decision-making*. London: Department of Health.

Duffy S & Gillespie J (2009) *Personalisation and Safeguarding*, version 1.1. London: In Control.

Personalisation: Practical thoughts and ideas from people making it happen   © OLM-Pavilion 2009

Personalisation and safeguarding adults

Lynn Laws

The 'personalisation' of public services through the Putting People First concordat in 2007 has raised a number of challenges for adult social care services, not least of which is safeguarding adults. How to develop and maintain robust safeguarding adults arrangements while increasing choice and control for individuals? The traditional patterns of care provision are no longer providing the universal service they once were. An increased menu of choice requires a greater range of services from which to choose, but much of this support, such as personal assistants or low-level preventative services, may not be subject to existing regulatory standards, nor the vetting requirements of the Safeguarding Vulnerable Groups Act (2006). Therefore, it is imperative that as local authorities transform their services, they examine their safeguarding adults arrangements, as increased choice and control for individuals brings with it an increased risk of abuse or exploitation. Greater control does not guarantee safety for individuals. Allowing greater personal choice and independence for the individual does not absolve the local authority from its responsibility, vicarious or otherwise.

Our work with a number of councils has identified a number of elements that need to be in place to ensure that the personalisation agenda does not leave individuals more vulnerable to abuse or exploitation. These are:

■ recognition that while the social services department has operational responsibility for safeguarding adults, including co-ordination of all the other agencies, it is the responsibility of the corporate body to ensure adequate safeguarding arrangements
■ clear corporate leadership, including elected members is essential
■ recognition that the responsibility of the local authority extends beyond those to whom it offers a direct service; an example of this would be 'self-funders' within a residential facility
■ a confident, competent and well trained frontline workforce that clearly understands that promoting the prevention of adult abuse and investigating any reported incidents is part of their core responsibility
■ a robust performance management system that enables the identification of trends and patterns of abuse

■ good quality assessments that include robust risk assessments of current and potential safeguarding issues followed by care plans that contain an agreed realistic risk management strategy.

Safeguarding should not be 'implemented' as a passive intervention for individuals, but rather as empowering and supporting people to protect themselves. This can be done in a range of ways:

■ raising the profile of safeguarding adults in the community and promoting community responsibility
■ providing meaningful and accessible public information to raise public awareness and understanding of safeguarding issues
■ working with individuals and groups to support them in upholding their right to live free from abuse or exploitation
■ ensuring a range of good quality, well publicised advocacy services are available, including independent mental capacity advocates where mental capacity may be an issue
■ ensuring that carers have access to assessments and a range of support services to alleviate stress and reduce circumstances where carers may become abusive
■ the establishment of accreditation processes for support provision by local authorities, and systems for facilitating CRB checks for people using individual/ personal budgets.

Individuals are at greater risk of abuse if they are socially isolated and not engaged with their local community. Changing life events can affect an individual's perceived status or social value in a community – death of a spouse, serious illness, financial difficulties. The risk of abuse can be reduced through strengthening communities and people's sense of citizenship. Personalisation, if implemented effectively with open systems and robust risk management, can be the way to achieve more effective safeguarding.

Chapter 8

A collection of key leaders' views on personalisation

Terry Dafter

Director, adult social care, Stockport Metropolitan Borough Council

The transformation of adult social care challenges all of us to think about the type of services we deliver and the information we provide to service users. It's a culture shift that will affect everyone's lives – within adult social services' staff, providers, the voluntary sector and, above all, service users and carers.

The issue of personalisation has involved heated debates among staff at conferences and seminars and is high on the agenda of all politicians involved in social care, being to some extent at the heart of new thinking about choice in public services. Sometimes though, I feel that we are in danger of creating a new set of acronyms and processes just as difficult as our current ones, indeed, never has so much jargon been coined by so few to confuse so many. Within Stockport we have had many debates about changing practices, implementing new processes, understanding the resource allocation system (RAS), the implications of brokerage and ensuring safeguarding. Crucially, we are also having these conversations with key partners, especially the NHS and crucially again with carers and users.

We need to start reaching out to everyone as early as possible. We need to bring people together to help them understand the changes and, moreover, the very real benefits of the transformation agenda.

Within the directorate we are running seminars, workshops and have set up an online interactive website called Stockport Voices, to help staff engage with the issues involved with the transformation agenda through the use of blogs run by senior managers, the voluntary sector and users and carers. The intention is to extend this during the next few months to include other stakeholders in the borough.

We're also completing another website – Quickheart – that will equip people across Stockport with better signposted information, helping service users with their decision-making, and giving them better quality information at the time they need it.

Current and future service users need to have the autonomy and control to help themselves – and that is difficult for people who are used to approaching us for a range of traditional services. The government has set a target for all local authorities by 2010 to have 30% of their service users using a form of self-directed support. That doesn't necessarily mean through a direct payment, but through other ways in terms of people knowing what their budget is and looking at how they may use that more creatively.

In Stockport that means we're looking at about 2,000 service users working towards this agenda, and that represents a major challenge for all of us. To achieve this it is my view that we need a fully qualified workforce and we are investing significantly in training our staff towards this end. This includes brokerage and support planning. We've made a commitment to qualified social workers to have a fully qualified workforce delivering this agenda with service users and carers.

All this work will only mean something, of course, if it makes a difference to people's lives. Generally, we are making measured and steady progress but in some areas we are really beginning to see the potential of the transformation agenda. Earlier this year, we launched a 12-month pilot for mental health services and by early 2010 we will have 60 people on self-directed support. This is proving highly popular and successful with users networking about the advantages of the new ways. This has meant that some people have come forward who were previously not interested in traditional services. It is also helping to keep people with complex needs at home and out of residential care or hospital. The aim is to look beyond the symptoms, beyond the illness, beyond the deficits, to think about people's strengths, people's hopes and people's aspirations, and how we can work together to achieve them.

These are genuinely exciting times for social care and in Stockport along with all other authorities we are looking at the transformation agenda as a key stepping stone to embedding real culture change in all of our services.

There is already a lot of very good practice going on in the borough, but we have to recognise that service users still tell us that they feel detached – they feel like patients, not people first and foremost, and that they continue to be dependent rather than empowered. While that situation remains, it is evident that we still have some way to go, but above all, personalisaton will be a significant way of starting to address that balance.

Personalisation: Practical thoughts and ideas from people making it happen   © OLM-Pavilion 2009

Jane Smith
Director, adult social services and housing, North Somerset Council

I think personalisation really has the potential to deliver improvements in quality of life, value for money and job satisfaction on a scale not seen before. Equally, however, there are many challenges and while the next two years will see major changes, we may not reach all the targets to which we aspire.

Launching personalisation in north Somerset went better than expected. With everything else we are doing, I was prepared for 'it's a good idea, but not now'. In fact, it was greeted positively, particularly by significant numbers of frontline staff as a refreshing opportunity to help carers and service users to take control of their lives and to make a difference. As one member of staff said, *'it reminds me why I came into this job in the first place'*. Another said, *'personalisation treats people as individuals rather than a set of needs'*.

Different parts of the service came together well to develop the strategy; finance, training and contracts staff organised training sessions. Volunteers came forward to develop the RAS and redesign business processes. Champions emerged from within the care management teams and have been enthusiastic in developing pilots across different client groups.

It has become much harder as we have started to implement it and it all takes longer than expected. Staff have begun to feel overloaded and we have had to delay some initiatives to keep the programme moving forward. Some performance indicators have deteriorated due to the increasing timescales of working through a new system and we are still wrestling with RAS and complex cases. Interestingly, some of the toughest challenges have been for staff 'letting go' and allowing the service users to develop their own support plans. Some of our care providers are very resistant to change, wanting to maintain the traditional models of care, and it feels as though we have much more to do to develop our local market.

Overall though, we are making progress. Implementation has given us the impetus to revisit some of our procedural and guidance frameworks, which needed updating. The response from NHS colleagues to personal health budgets has been very enthusiastic and we are preparing a joint bid.

Most importantly there are some heartening case studies showing how people feel personal budgets have changed their lives. We have been fortunate that our Partnerships for Older People Projects (POPP) programme helped us begin to pilot personal budgets with carers earlier and we have built on this experience. Although the (TSC) grant is limited, it has enabled us to put improved infrastructure in place and to

give staff important development opportunities. It has also been – and continues to be – helpful to have access to OLM advice and resources and to share problems, but also to learn from others through our regional network.

Mel Cassedy
Strategic business manager, adults and communities services, Suffolk County Council

The way we deliver adult social care services is changing rapidly, and for the better. The personalisation agenda puts people firmly in the driving seat, with the government and local authorities acknowledging that the customer is best placed to take the decisions to direct their own care and support.

We have a once-in-a-generation opportunity to embrace this major shift in responsibility. With Suffolk being by no means unusual in seeing rising numbers of people needing care and living longer, and at a time when public funding is severely constrained for the foreseeable future, we must find new ways not only of living within our means but also improving people's well-being and quality of life.

I know that self-directed support makes sense. Our customers have seen huge benefits already from using direct payments: from taking greater freedom and control to direct their own lives, to the creativity to go to the cinema for respite care, or pay for the online shopping delivery charge, to use just two examples.

Personal budgets herald a new age in transparent government. For the first time, we are not only able to tell people how much money we are spending on them – this becomes an integral part of the care they receive. The power is shifting away from people's dependency on the local authority to decide what they need, to an empowered society making their own choices and managing their resources. With this, however, come potential risks to vulnerable people. These risks are of concern to councils and the regulatory bodies, and they need to be mitigated without compromising or diluting customer independence and choice.

I am aware of the challenges we face. Delivering quality services with less money will not be easy, nor will self-directed support be the answer to everything. To make sure we get it right, and make the most of the opportunities that we and our customers have, we must support our staff through this significant period of change.

Self-directed support represents a significant culture change for the community, our staff, partner agencies and private and voluntary sectors. There is no magic solution for changing what we do overnight, but so far I have seen some positive responses to this agenda and the willingness to work together to get it right from the start.

One indication of where this is succeeding is with organisations representing family carers. We have worked with three such organisations recently to deliver a series of engagement sessions with their staff and trustees. The emphasis was firmly given to partnership, and approaching the self-directed support agenda together. By working collectively to get this engagement early on we have shared ownership – essential when collaboration with our partners is so vital.

On a broader scale, I keep a close eye on national developments. We have learnt a lot from the pilot authorities and the pioneering approaches taken to develop personalisation across the country. I think local authorities have much to offer from their own experiences, and I would encourage this sharing of best practice so that we can learn from one another.

Personalisation represents a challenging but bright future, and one we should be welcoming with collectively open arms.

Jo Cleary
Executive director of adults' and community services,
London Borough of Lambeth

In recent months there has been a lot of activity around personalisation and developing personalised services in Lambeth aimed at council staff and service users.

For instance, in and around Lambeth there has been a poster campaign running telling the story of how personalised services are being developed and what it means, so people in the borough can buy into it.

We have also been doing a lot of work at staff conferences, including playing a DVD that showed stories of people whose lives had changed through the work we had done to date.

This builds on what we have been doing within the council where we have been working on the personalisation agenda for some time. I initially led this, but now Jamie Nevin, who was appointed as director of personalising services in July 2008, is leading the agenda within the council.

His appointment provides someone at a very senior level with the responsibility to lead the agenda, because it is going to affect every part of the council in time and some people underestimate that. They think it will just affect social care, but it will actually involve our HR systems, commissioning systems, payroll – everything.

Jamie and his team are now working hard on building the infrastructure for this as one of the six corporate priorities for the council.

In Control

A major part of personalisation is introducing individual budgets for service users to arrange their own care. Lambeth was part of the In Control pilot of individual budgets and this has been very successful. Lambeth currently has 30 people with learning disabilities and complex needs with a budget and more in the process of applying for one.

One of our main successes has been Sean Davis (see: http://www.in-control.org.uk/ site/INCO/Templates/General.aspx?pageid=870&cc=GB), who is 22 and has cerebral palsy and is partially sighted. Sean's mother, Sandra, has used the individual budget to employ personal assistants that are around his own age who can relate to him and help him to do what he wants to and take more control over his life.

Indeed, Sandra is such an advocate of individual budgets that she has agreed to become a carer's champion, working with us for two days a week on secondment from her regular job, to help sell it to carers and service users.

We are now planning to roll individual budgets out to other service user groups and hope to repeat the initial successes on a broader scale. We will also offer an individual budget to all young people making the transition from children's to adult services.

As part of this, we will be using a new resource allocation system – RAS 5 – from June. This has been developed following an extensive consultation with providers, users, carers and our workforce to ensure it provides the right outcomes for service users.

Aims of personalisation

Ultimately, we want to see that people are changing their lives through individual budgets. It may not be huge numbers in the first years, but we are effecting a big culture shift over time, involving everyone, but particularly communities; we need to get our local communities on board with this.

It goes back to the old days of communities; when you hear personalised stories, such as people saying 'I've got my next door neighbour to give me driving lessons' that is a completely different way of delivering services that wasn't happening in inner London before – people don't talk to their neighbours at the moment.

This also includes using resources in and around the community that people might not associate with care services. It is about looking at what we offer across the board – such as leisure, libraries and the arts – that could be of interest to service users and what would make a difference to their lives.

But personalisation is also about taking away the paternalism that's always been around in social work. My message to social workers is that we are in a high-risk business – we always have been – but personalisation is about enabling service users to take calculated risks. We facilitate them to take more control over their own lives, it is as simple as that.

However, you have to measure the risk. Our role is to make sure we create a safety net around the arrangements that enable them to lead their lives to the fullest.

Some people may be sceptical and say personalisation is just another fad, but it isn't because it is at a grass roots level; it is changing services from the bottom up and that's the major difference.

Lorna Campbell
Lambeth Council's cabinet member for health and care services

It is clear to me that personalisation is the way forward for social care, primarily because it gives people increased choice in the services and support they receive. Current care packages are very 'health weighted', with little emphasis on the person as a whole.

From my point of view, personalisation offers a number of clear benefits. For example, as I get older, it could become harder for me to pursue my interests. I enjoy going to the theatre, but if my health begins to deteriorate, I might not be able to go as often as I'd like.

Now, it would be great if I could include something in my care package to say that provided I still had all my faculties and could still enjoy it, I could go to the theatre once a month accompanied by somebody else.

I'm sure it would greatly improve my quality of life, and it would also feed into the whole preventative agenda.

Lambeth's experience

In Lambeth, our experience of personalisation began with an In Control individual budget pilot, which focused on people with learning disabilities. As a result, we've already been able to identify potential challenges that we will need to overcome if we are to make this programme a success.

For example, there are some people who don't want to manage their own budgets and there are some people who would want to but can't – so we have to look at the logistics of this and consider how we're going to make it happen.

We've also been liaising with the London Borough of Barking and Dagenham, and their experience of personalisation is very different to ours. Their pilot ran across the whole spectrum of learning disabilities and older people's services. But demographically speaking, Lambeth is markedly different to Barking and Dagenham and it made far more sense for them to go for it.

So we've still got to roll this initiative out across older people's services, and I'm sure other issues will arise as we do this.

A slow process

The thing is, because personalisation is innovative and new you can't rush it. There are a number of different groups responsible for implementing the agenda, and you have to ensure that the workforce is fully prepared and ready to deliver the initiative. There's so much that needs to be done, I don't think we can go at it at top speed because if we're not properly organised then the agenda will fail.

We've got to consider the staff issues, then we have to consider how the third sector is going to be affected by personalisation, and we've also got service users and clients, and we need to look at how they are going to be affected too.

I'm sure some service users are concerned that they are going to lose out, or feel that this is another way for the council to avoid its responsibility to people living in the borough. So we've got to iron out all of these issues as well.

We need to get everyone around the same table to discuss these things, and getting that general consensus takes time – which is a concern.

However, despite these challenges, I still think personalisation is a good thing.

Jeff Jerome
National director, social care transformation, ADASS

When the aims of the personalisation agenda were first outlined in *Putting People First* back in 2007, it was billed as heralding the transformation of adult social care – to meet the demographic challenges of an aging society and to deliver much greater individual choice and control.

Now, more than a year into the implementation of the programme, evidence of that transformation is becoming apparent, with many councils seeing progress towards more personalised services and changed processes, according to a recent ADASS/ LGA survey.

Indeed, the survey said four out of five local authorities feel that the range and flexibility of provision has already improved, and more than three-quarters believe that the development of preventative services in their area has had a significant impact on outcomes.

In addition, more than 93,000 people had a personal budget by the end of March, equating to more than £681 million of council expenditure. However, the majority of these personal budgets have come from a minority of councils. This is due to some councils deciding to develop other parts of the personalisation agenda, such as preventative services, or preparing a new operational model before implementing personal budgets.

However, in councils that have done this, commissioners and strategic directors now need to pay more attention to developing personal budgets. The places that haven't really started properly allocating budgets to people have a lot of catching-up to do over the next 20 months or so to 2011. But this should not be at the expense of other parts of the personalisation agenda; it is important that all aspects are focused on for the agenda to realise its potential for service users.

For example, for personal budgets to be truly effective, a wider market offering needs to be in place. If service users, even with personal budgets, are still going to get the same sort of services and buy the same things that were there when the council was organising it, you haven't gone very far. It is important to develop market choice as well, and to establish services to support people as they make choices in that market.

But, to ensure an effective wider market offering, commissioners need to engage with others. There is a commissioning responsibility to engage with providers and to check out the likely wants and needs of the population – people who are going to get personal budgets and people using their own money – to make sure those things are there. A commissioner's job is to shape and enable market development rather than drive it through using financial muscle.

Peter Hay
Strategic director, adults and communities, Birmingham City Council
Personalisation should be viewed as an opportunity to develop more innovative responses that will help our council rise to the challenges of providing effective social care services within the available budget.

While Birmingham's population profile is not aging as quickly as it is in some other areas, the make-up of the population – and in particular, its poor health – mean that the council's social care costs will grow slightly above the national average, according to a London School of Economics survey.

With funding tight – and likely to get tighter – the chance to be more innovative in commissioning services is timely.

We, at Birmingham City Council, could either have continued with the traditional response of altering eligibility criteria, which would have some impact on that gap between cost and likely income, or we could do something very different. For us, personalisation is not just a set of issues about rights, which are very important, but it is also about trying to set out a different way of making sure that we can have world-class services that we can afford, within the context of the demography and needs that we've got.

For instance, along with personal budgets, Birmingham City Council is also seeking to pool departmental budgets, such as learning disability and mental health – what I term as 'one public purse' approach – to meet often shared needs.

Another key part of achieving this is through being more transparent about how resources are being used. This is about engaging with service users, self-funders, and the broader community about how councils are commissioning and delivering services; and it is about what the choices are and how they are being made within the money available.

Value for money

For instance, there are plans – which have caused some controversy – to close a number of day services in Birmingham, but I believe the money can be better used elsewhere – and once service users are aware of the financial situation, they agree.

When you start saying to service users 'this day care facility costs £50 per day ... is that worth £50 a day?' Quite a lot are saying back to us 'what could I do with £50 a day – something different.'

The heart of personalisation is not necessarily about direct payments or personal budgets, it is about sharing the responsibility for getting value for the public pound and enabling the service user to be central to that objective.

That, I think, particularly in recession times, is absolutely key to it. It's not about 'we know best about what constitutes value and quality and use of the public pound', but it is a shared journey with the service user at the heart of it, saying 'I think, for £50 a day, I could do better and hand you back money'.

Personalisation: Practical thoughts and ideas from people making it happen   © OLM-Pavilion 2009

Recession effect

Getting better value for money has become more of a priority thanks to the recession; it has already forced people to be realistic about how – or if – the gap between the costs of care and likely income is to be bridged.

The recession has taken away even the faint residual hope that some people might have had that the gap between care costs and income would be closed by increased public spending.

However, this was never a realistic expectation – the way money is spent would always have had to change to ensure that the most is made of available resources.

Indeed, it has put more emphasis on the challenges of meeting substantially increased demand, rising expectations, and the insistence of self-funders that they are not ignored by the state, after having paid a lifetime of taxes – all from a limited pot of funds.

The recession has thrown into sharper focus the scale of the challenge we face to make sure that we're delivering on that economic side of personalisation without damaging its value base, its roots, its anchoring in choice and control.

Effects on staff

The value base of personalisation, with its focus on giving service users choice and control in their lives, is something that many of the social care workforce have welcomed.

Broadly, the majority of staff are very supportive, the value base fits with their reasons for coming into social care, but for others, it just does not.

Managing those that do not agree with the concept is a big challenge, though. While some people come round to it, others remain opposed. In those cases, staff have to be managed sensitively, including, in some cases, finding other areas where their skills and experiences can be used.

But while the majority of staff welcome the philosophy, it still requires a culture change – and additional training – for them to implement the agenda on the ground. The training for our staff is not technically based; it is there to ensure understanding of the different values and approaches that individual budgets will demand of them.

That applies throughout the whole system, including my role and what it will demand of me, in relation to that broader debate and to the whole value we put around choice and control.

Future

Personalisation is a long-term agenda for social care, but it will also soon begin to have a more pronounced effect on other council departments. Personalisation is putting in place a set of values that have a broader application and I think you can see that emerging in political thinking. As we're entering a period of considering what the policies will be for the general election, you can see the personalisation concept beginning to be thought about across a broader spectrum.

For example, there are plans to pilot individual budgets in health care – Birmingham has potential pilot status for this. You can see how the concept can be taken forward; and I think it can be very much rooted in how we manage what will be difficult times, economically, by having clarity about what you get for your pound.

For commissioners, the challenges are about shaping the market, but, more and more, it will be in collaboration, not just with service users and carers, but with other authorities. Increasingly, we are going to be looking at cross-boundary approaches between local authorities, particularly in specialised markets like learning disability residential care; how do we understand and have a common view and even share some of our approaches to those markets?

Dawn Warwick

Director of adult social services, Wandsworth

We've decided to fully embrace the transformation agenda in Wandsworth, as it presents a real opportunity to make a difference to people's lives. But we're not going into this half-heartedly – we've produced a three-year transformation programme that will completely change social care delivery in Wandsworth.

The programme contains detailed plans to address the systems that need to change; the organisational structure that we need to put in place to support this, and the cultural change – the attitudes, behaviours and approaches from staff.

To prepare for this, we've spent 18 months working closely with CSED (Care Services Efficiency Delivery) in the Department of Health to help eliminate bureaucracy, and we've now got a strong foundation on which to start building the personalisation programme.

We've adopted a 'learn as we go' approach to the agenda. We've decided not to design a system, a process and a structure, and then just roll it out with a big bang because, going by the experiences of other councils, they get some parts right but not others.

Personalisation: Practical thoughts and ideas from people making it happen   © OLM-Pavilion 2009

Instead, we've identified 100 people across all service user areas – older people, people with mental health problems, people with learning disabilities and people with physical disabilities – and we're going to test the resource allocation system (RAS) and the self-assessment questionnaire that we've devised.

Our aim is to create a common RAS that is appropriate for all client groups – we don't want an individual RAS for learning disabilities, one for mental health and one for older people. That may mean we have to look at how we structure the points system, but we want a simple system that is transparent and works for all client groups.

Engaging with staff

We've already started to have preliminary conversations with staff about the three-year programme, and we're looking for them to come to us with ideas and possibilities.

To facilitate this, we've got a blog on the council's intranet site that features various topics and conversations on the programme. We also ran a number of awareness-raising workshops last autumn, which about 300 members of staff attended.

The response to the transformation agenda has been mixed. I think some people are really excited by personalisation and some people are worried by it. Even the feedback we've been getting hasn't always been positive – but we need to hear the bad as well as the good. The benefit of this approach is that there are a lot of interesting suggestions and ideas coming forward.

The trick has been to encourage the excited staff members and harness them to champion it, but not to be too zealous and overbearing with others. It's been about getting the balance right.

Back to the future

Although what we're trying to achieve is something new, I think in some ways it is going back to what we did 20 or 30 years ago, in terms of cutting out the bureaucracy.

This means we can get rid of the 30-page assessment forms and get people completing their own self-assessments about what they feel would make their lives better.

Andrew McCulloch
Chief executive, Mental Health Foundation

Personalisation raises a number of challenges for social care providers, some of which cross client groups. One of these is making the opportunities it provides accessible to people who experience mental health problems or have a learning disability.

Whether there are psychological barriers involved, or a fluctuating or more permanent lack of capacity, some people may need a good deal of impartial advice and advocacy to reach decisions about what care they want, and how to get it. In the evaluation of the individual budgets pilot scheme, mental health service users who participated reported significantly higher quality of life, and people with learning disabilities were more likely to feel that they had control over their daily lives. So it can be done, but it will only happen if the right support is widely available. Failure to do so risks increasing inequity, as those who have the skills to operate the new system will receive all the benefits.

Three challenges facing providers stand out. First, they must be very clear what personalisation actually means, both for their own staff, and in their dealings with commissioners and clients (who will increasingly be one and the same). Clients and care staff may fairly readily understand the concept of choice and control. However, the varying use of terms such as 'personalisation', 'direct payments', 'individual budgets', 'co-production', 'personalised care planning' and 'self-directed support' (to choose a few) are creating confusion.

Personalisation is about much more than personal budgets and requires a significant cultural change in how staff work, to enable clients to be genuine partners in care. The Department of Health has talked about 'the need to win the hearts and minds of frontline staff' (Department of Health, 2008) and providers will need to ensure that their staff are wholly on board with this new vision.

Second, providers will need to be more flexible about how they offer services. While many clients may actually prefer to receive services in a traditional way, an increasing number will seek greater control over their own budgets and commission their own care. This poses challenges for organisations in three significant areas:

- planning and managing their workforce
- managing and reporting on quality
- budgeting and collecting money from many individual customers.

Third, commissioners have their own challenge in finding the right range and quality of providers to meet the needs of individuals and wider local populations. All providers, whether large or small, statutory, voluntary or independent, will be operating in an increasingly competitive market with new entrants at both ends of the scale. Existing

providers who fail to adapt services to what clients want risk losing both clients and staff. At the same time, there will be new opportunities for organisations that are able to be very nimble and flexible and can focus holistically on clients. Only then will the rhetoric of personalisation become a reality for clients hoping to achieve real increases in their quality of life.

Reference

Department of Health (2008) *Transforming Social Care*. Local authority circular. London: Department of Health.

Lord Victor Adebowale CBE
CEO of Turning Point

Personalisation, if implemented correctly will be incredibly beneficial to both service users and providers within the health and social care sector. Not only does it put control back in the hands of the individual but it also gives us the opportunity to do things differently for our clients, which is very exciting. However, despite personalisation being high on the political agenda, there is a long way to go before it is translated into a reality.

Currently, personalisation is moving more swiftly in disability and care for older people services, than in other areas. However, personalisation can and should be extended to other sectors. At the last meeting of the All Party Parliamentary Group on People with Complex Needs and Dual Diagnosis, which Turning Point administers, politicians and representatives from various health and social care organisations discussed what personalisation will mean for people with complex needs in the areas of mental health and substance misuse. Turning Point provides services in the fields of learning disability, mental health and substance misuse and we are looking closely at ways of implementing the personalisation agenda across all three of our main sectors.

There are several implications of the personalisation agenda that have raised concerns and which do need to be looked at in more detail. The idea of clients employing untrained personal assistants under the new system of individual budgets raises alarm bells for many but whilst some form of regulation is certainly needed, it's important that we don't deny our service users the greater level of choice and control that individual budgets can bring.

Individual budgets will no doubt have implications for frontline staff. They will need to be a lot more flexible, for example, if a client requires support during the night. As individual budgets come into effect, people will be able to approach health care providers with a care plan and budget and ask us how we will be able to deliver that plan. We must therefore be able to communicate to clients exactly which services are on offer and signpost them through the system accordingly. Staff may also see

a change in their day-to-day role depending on the wishes of the client and service managers and will need a greater understanding of the individual costs of their services so they can share these with commissioners and self-funding individuals.

When people are given personal budgets and have more choice over which services they use, the emphasis on value for money will be even greater. Social enterprises have always been focused on delivering maximum outcome for minimum costs. However, personalisation means all health care providers will need to raise their game, offering more creative and cost-effective services.

Personalisation brings with it some uncertainty but also the potential to empower and change lives for the better. Personal budgets will mean individuals will be able to purchase services from more than one provider and could revolutionise support for those with complex needs by avoiding the problem of services being commissioned in silos. If health care commissioners and providers work together on this then we have every reason to believe it can work.

Chapter 9

Personalisation and mental health

Nick Dixon and Tony Bennett

The Stockport Mental Health Self-directed Support Project builds upon a maintained focus on addressing the culture of the mental health trust and other service providers here in Stockport over the last five years. This project is seen as a pragmatic way of embedding culture change and transforming social care practice within a secondary mental health service, driven by commissioners, service users and carers.

Our team had a track record of being committed to the principles and values of self-directed support not least in the following:

- a focus on values-based awareness to sit alongside evidenced-based practice
- the organisation of a Stockport Recovery Network of champions of recovery based in every service and team alongside people who use services, and carers
- a mental health joint commissioning strategy and action plan that has the adoption of the recovery approach as its first recommendation and the creation of a number of recovery focused services (the Stockport Well-being Centre, the Stockport MIND Crisis Accommodation and Home Support Service, for example).

However, we wanted to go further and really explore the potential of adopting a self-directed support approach. Not least because service users and carers repeatedly ask for more hope-inspiring services to be made available, for services that recognise their strengths, knowledge and potential that don't focus on their symptoms alone, and for there to be meaningful engagement about what matters to people as well as what is wrong. This recovery agenda is happening but it was very clear to many of us that self-directed support could offer the opportunity to further this agenda in a very dramatic and powerful way.

The Self-directed Support (SDS) Project was launched in February 2009. It seeks to engage at least 60 people who use services in the year ahead with the In Control model of SDS. Members of the early intervention team and other champions of recovery from across mental health service teams, including older age community mental health teams, have received training in recovery tools and person-centred planning in preparation. Pathways of how the self assessment questionnaire (SAQ) and the resource allocation system (RAS) sit alongside the new care programme approach (CPA) have been worked up and guidance has been written.

A third sector organisation, Step By Step, has been brought in to build capacity within teams and among service users themselves for the tasks of brokerage, with a focus on individual and peer support planning. The two brokers involved are supporting staff to see the potential that can be released by self-directed support, described as not only thinking outside the box but living outside of it. The brokers are quickly establishing a rapport with the social workers and nurses, many of whom are already embracing this new way of working.

What is interesting to see is the impact on the supply side when people themselves have real influence over services – by being able to choose whether or not to invest their personal budget into them. Given how powerful peers can be when acting as ambassadors of hope to people struggling to overcome their mental distress, early successes have been achieved through the establishment of two recovery programmes run at the Stockport Well-being Centre, which are accessible to people with their personal budgets.

'Thrivers' offers its attendees the tools needed to turn lives around; introduced by Mike Smith and Marion Aslan from Crazy Diamond (www.crazydiamond.org.uk), this programme has been so successful it is now to be run twice a week for people to access at any time.

'I hope Thrivers has a long life and will continue to help others come from the dark into the light.' Attendee, March 2009

For those needing the security of a closed group and more easily established peer support, the development of a service user and carer social enterprise, a community interest company called Accentuate the Positive, has been an early success. This small group of users and carers was already offering values training to staff from the foundation trust. Now, as they establish their own enterprise, they are offering their own course known as RAPT (recovery action and awareness planning training). It is hoped that through RAPT and Thrivers, alongside the growth of peer support networks, there will develop peer commissioning of services through the pooling of personal budgets.

As with other self-directed support projects, the notion of an easily accessible budget to fund one-off items linked to outcomes has quickly shown its value. For instance, the idea of a 'recovery budget', an easily accessed pot of money for the purchase of single

items such as a bicycle or a laptop; these direct payments will be made with minimum bureaucracy and maximum speed on provision of evidence of how such an item may support a journey of recovery. Already the budget has supported the purchase of art materials to encourage a former artist to begin his work again following his loss of confidence, the purchase of horse riding equipment (horse riding lessons will shortly be purchased through the personal budget) and the printing of a life story novel, a powerful book that has the potential to support many others as well as the individual's belief in his future as an author and recovery ambassador.

An interesting development we are now looking at is the 'human recovery budget', again one-off accessible payments, but rather than funding material goods, the budget will be used to fund time with members of Accentuate the Positive. The thinking behind this is that short time spent with peers who have 'been there' and recovered may motivate others to take the first steps to being in control of their recovery pathway in a more effective way than a paid worker could do.

There are now, at week 10, 17 service users on the project with personal budgets. Many continue to hang on to their traditional services, not yet ready to take down the scaffolding that traditional services have built around them to maintain their mental health but most are planning to use their remaining budget for more creative services. Interestingly, some of the budgets are being used to fund the 'extras' that address quality of life, such as the young man attending karate lessons for whom the day centre was never a serious option, or the keen astronomer who is advertising at the local astronomy society for a personal companion to talk about the wider meaning of life with. An early success is the long-term day centre service user who enjoyed the gardening group that met once a week for an hour or two; he now has his own allotment, shed, tools and the means to buy in gardening advice, able to visit and tend to it at his own choice. Successes are already refreshingly evident, the purchase of a bicycle and equipment has already enabled one man to return to his own flat to live. Having been too anxious to travel on the bus to visit his mother, he had chosen to stay with her and not go out; he is now attending college on his bicycle. One lady who used the recovery budget to buy a laptop to support her interest in animation and to support a college course she now intends to take up, declined the offer of internet connection saying, *'If I have it I know I won't go out and that wont be good for me'*. Service users, like the rest of us, know what works for them.

The project is being evaluated by the University of Chester and will inform commissioners of the most effective ways of delivering the facets of SDS as well as evidencing positive outcomes through collated narratives. Research questions will include mapping where and how users spend their resources, what the characteristics of different brokerage systems are and what the most effective processes within those

systems of brokerage are. Outcome narratives are essential to win the hearts and minds of practitioners and those service users who hold to traditional service delivery. With the support of OLM-Pavilion, the development of a local Stockport Mental Health Care Knowledge internet site with planned weekly video blogs, will support this process. Already two service users with personal budgets have taken possession of the small video cameras, intent on capturing the difference that self-directed support has made to their lives and that of their families and friends. The recruitment of a service user to work with the technology to capture the outcomes is now planned.

The establishment of a risk enablement panel has been seen as a crucial step to gain the confidence of care co-ordinators. Positive risk taking is to be supported but the natural anxiety of the staff, if called upon to support an unwise decision, is probably the most obvious barrier to changing the focus of service delivery from one where a professional knows best to one that is truly self-determining. The panel will be a way of supporting practitioners to carry risk that they may feel reluctant to support alone, given positive risk taking is at the heart of empowerment and personal growth. Self-determination inevitably carries greater risk, if someone isn't allowed to make unwise decisions and learn from their consequences, in reality how empowering is the service? We all learn from our mistakes, it is how we grow. What this project seeks to do is to address the balance of services that so often 'warehouse' people, keep them safe but dependent and often hopeless. This does not negate the absolute duty of services to manage risk safely, this remains at the forefront of all involved in this project; it does mean that there is more dialogue and equality in decision-making between the expert in their situation and experience, and the expert by their training and knowledge. Interestingly, at the end of week 10 of the project, the panel has yet to meet but there are already care co-ordinators who are willing to testify to the different results already being seen through personalisation.

Lincolnshire

You will read stories in this book about how people's lives have been changed by the use of personal budgets. I celebrate those changes and recognise that stories are a powerful way of changing attitudes. I want to share in my contribution the success stories not of service users, but of practitioners who have also had their working lives transformed by self-directed support. I am indebted to the award-winning Skegness and Louth Community Mental Health Recovery Teams for permission to use their material here. I will try and faithfully describe their self-directed support journey – their ambition to create 'major change to the way in which the two teams deliver social care services', and how this 'dramatically changed the way that the team worked' – powerful stuff.

The teams were already familiar with the use of direct payments, which had provided flexibility to the people they were working with. However, they wanted to go further.

Their journey began with a series of awareness-raising events, which focused on putting empowered service users at the core of the process. At the outset the prognosis was not favourable.

'The first thing we noted from the start of this project was the scepticism, reluctance and even hostility many staff had towards the concept of personalisation.'

The team noted some of the reasons why this attitude prevailed, concluding that they, *'demonstrate the deep and entrenched levels of professional, managerial and organisational resistance to the principles of personalisation in the early days of the pilot'*.

However, the teams were aware of the artificiality of separating out the 'well' and the 'unwell', being very aware of the very real risks that all of us face to our mental health, and how small events can bring great change. They talk of *'a very thin dividing line indeed between who we are as professionals and becoming a 'service user'. It only takes an accident, a mental health breakdown etc, and we move from one to the other, yet our need to have control in our lives and to have dignity and respect remains'*.

The team was aware of a major culture shift that was necessitated by a new way of thinking, and the contrast between a support plan and a care plan, and the attendant concerns by professionals about a lack of control. They also worried about risk both health and financial.

All in all they describe an unlikely scenario from which radical change could come about, but amazingly this did transform the way whole teams worked, and the attitude of those team members, which underpinned that change. All of this leads to the marked improvement in the choice and control of the people they were working with, and directly to improved health and well-being. Let's explore how this came about.

As part of a pilot process, which was in a constant state of flux, it is apparent to me that there were four key aspects that kept this journey live:

- the development and constant revision of systems and ways of working to provide a consistent administrative framework
- the commitment and dedication of the team members whose fire was fanned by the benefits that they saw in people's lives
- the realisation that most of their clients were very able to define the outcomes that they wanted for their own lives, and were creative in so doing
- the understanding that individual budgets could make differences to people's lives in ways that traditional services could not.

The changes that these things brought about engendered a team spirit, which seems to have affected all of those team members. They say:

'The pilot led to all the care co-ordinators pulling together as a team and learning from our collective experiences; being a pilot site for such an important development led to a feeling of pride and, for once, being able to put Skegness on the map, so to speak. Those with any knowledge of Skegness will know that regrettably it has had very little to put it on the map in recent years. The decline in mining and northern manufacturing industry and the rise of the package holiday presaged a decline in its standing from which it is still striving to recover.'

I trust that this very brief story of two teams' efforts, and the positive change that it has engendered will be a fitting balance to the success stories you will have heard about individuals and their transformed lives. I will leave the conclusion to the team who so kindly donated this material:

'Personal budgets have the potential to change lives in an unprecedented and empowering way. For care co-ordinators, individual budgets offer an opportunity for a unique collaboration with service users to rediscover (or perhaps discover) creative and radical ways of working with people with mental illness.'

Chapter 10

Personalisation and developing people

Alex MacNeil and Joolz Casey

In this chapter we will look at a new way to approach the issues of workforce development in the social care system. First, we will look at new thinking and issues and then we will move on to some useful tools.

Personalisation relies on a radical shift in our perspectives of the purpose of the social care system. We must change our thinking from professionals who design and deliver services **for** people. We are moving to a place where people are not seen as 'service users' – but equal partners in the best way to use the money available to them to get a better life.

When we are approaching workforce development, it is crucial that we keep this different perspective in mind from the start. It is the same shift, which in self-directed support, takes an individual from being the passive recipient of services, to a full and active citizen. In terms of workforce, or learning and development, this translates into individuals being equal partners, both in learning and providing expertise, and crucially requires those of us who have been responsible for commissioning learning and qualifications to be able to respond in a more individual and flexible way to what people say is important for them. When we consider the outcomes for the development of new professional roles and qualifications, we must do so in a way that equally balances the professional development of the worker, with the minimum statutory learning, and what's important for the person receiving support. (see **figure 2: The balanced learning model**).

This is a new foundation from which to approach workforce development in social care. Without it, we will continue to rely on our system of employer led qualification structure that won't reflect what people controlling their own budgets will want or be able to buy.

Workforce development in social care traditionally takes place from a professional's perspective. Non-professional people are rarely considered experts. There are exceptions; people who use services are much more likely to be involved in or leading the delivery of training to staff. But it remains a continuing problem of how to fund training for anyone who isn't considered to be part of the paid, registered, social care workforce.

Personalisation brings a new way of making the social care system work – a new way of doing things not only for the paid professionals who we traditionally think of when we think 'workforce', but also for the hundreds of thousands of people who are waiting for better lives as a result.

New thinking and the issues

From 'workforce development' to 'developing people'

For people to be able to lead their lives as full and active citizens, we, the workforce development 'experts' in social care, must support the learning and development of many more people than just paid, registered professionals.

In our three circles model (see **figure 1**), individuals and their families are seen as equally important in our consideration of who needs to learn what about personalisation. We believe that separating out the workforce development needs of the professionals from this group and wider community is a mistake and is likely to lead to the development of strategies and training programmes in isolation of understanding the real outcomes in people's lives.

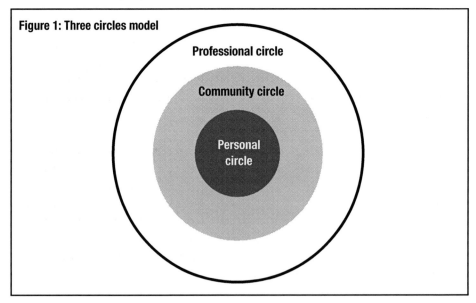

Figure 1: Three circles model

Professional circle

Community circle

Personal circle

Personalisation: Practical thoughts and ideas from people making it happen   © OLM-Pavilion 2009

The circles emphasise the fact that the best learning relies on good relationships rather than just technical expertise. The relationships between the three circles are as important as the people and activity included within them.

This way of looking at developing people for social care challenges us to consider the workforce development of one circle in relation to the others. It is a reminder that unless we consider the whole picture, we will not develop a strategic, person-centred approach to workforce development.

If we continue to concentrate only on the traditional social care workforce, we will repeat the mistakes of the past in which we have concentrated our financial and human resources on developing a group of skilled professionals, taught by other skilled professionals. The well-meant creation of these skilled professionals results in:

- the overall professionalism of people's lives
- increased dependency on professional services
- decreasing natural support and community activity
- the lack of available funds for people who are micro-employers, either for their own development, or the development of the people they employ to support them. (Poll & Duffy, 2008)

These assertions are challenging and can be backed up by significant numbers of personal testimonies but are not easy to back up with formal research. This is because the outcomes of qualifications such as NVQs and national minimum standards have not been clearly measured against the lives of people being supported.

The personal circle

The personal circle includes the individual who needs support and the people who are important to them, usually friends and family. This circle represents a largely untapped source of knowledge and expertise. This group of people are also the group of people who have not been included in our traditional approach to social care, having been seen as service users rather than employers or resource controllers.

The exchange of learning between this and the other circles should be extensive. However, the challenge in accomplishing this lies not only in the protective attitudes of some professionals, but also in the sense of learned helplessness of some families and individuals. Being at the end of the professional gift model (Duffy, 2006) can sometimes have a profoundly disempowering effect on people who struggle to see themselves as experts in their own lives. This is a radical shift in thinking for many people. There are families and individuals in this group who currently see themselves as clients and want to be in, as they see it, the strong and capable hands of caring experts. It is hard to feel like a valued expert when professionals have for years told you that you are not.

Part of any developing people strategy for personalisation must be to support links with people who do see themselves as experts and are keen to share their own expertise as they develop the confidence and skills in others.

This approach can be summarised by considering what we are moving from, and what we are moving towards.

Moving from	Moving towards
Professionals know best what training people need.	Self-direction becomes stronger the more the individual and those who know and care for them are seen as the primary source of guidance and support.
The only valued learning is professionally accredited learning.	

The community circle

The community circle includes not only people's local communities but also wider society. It is naïve to expect that by concentrating learning solely within the social care sector, we can support the massive changes that are needed for people to become and remain active citizens.

The findings of the Ibsen report (Glendinning *et al*, 2008) and the In Control Phase 3 report (Poll & Duffy, 2008) both demonstrate that when people have control of their own money, they are able to live fuller lives and be part of their own communities. The outcomes of personalisation therefore will include an impact in our communities and this shouldn't be ignored in the context of developing people.

However, there is a risk that a poorly thought out training plan for the community creates a barrier between people and their communities, with community members believing that they need professional training before being ready to include people. Our aim must be to make sure that ordinary relationships are established and encouraged, introducing technical expertise only when it is needed.

In their recent research briefing for SCIE, Needham and Carr (2009) introduce an interesting evidence base for co-production in adult social care. Put simply, when power is properly shared with individuals and families (what we call simply, partnership working), it leads to better outcomes for people in their communities. We are talking about proper, power sharing partnerships, as opposed to the ways we have included people via consultation and participation strategies to date. It's not always simple to recognise when something is participative in a tokenistic way and when something is truly developed in partnership. The test has to be whether power has been shared and

meaningful change achieved. Often, and as we are seeing in adult social care, true partnership working requires significant changes to the systems within an organisation.

An example of partnership working between the professional and personal circles resulting in an impact in the community circle can be seen in Oldham. A man who has a disability used some of his individual budget to convert his car so that he could become a disabled driving instructor. He has subsequently not found it easy to find clients. Clearly, in this situation, the sensible solution in terms of learning should be to support him as a small business, rather than to try to teach people in the community about disability awareness. This sort of small business support for micro enterprises should be a feature of your developing people plans.

The issues remain within this circle.

- What learning can we share and stimulate so that personalisation becomes an important and personal issue for everyone, not just the people who use the social care system?
- What will it take for communities to be fully inclusive, to support and be supported by people who have traditionally been excluded from them?

The professional circle

This circle includes all social care professionals, including direct supporters (personal assistants and support workers), social workers, and commissioners. It also includes health professionals.

Much of the focus to date on workforce development for personalisation has been to focus on the changing role of the social worker and the requirements of an emerging personal assistant workforce.

We have met many social workers involved in personalisation who report a return to the values of social work, a sense of being empowered themselves to use the system to then empower people to get better lives. But equally, there is the fear, anxiety and mistrust you would expect when people are facing change on this scale. There are practitioners and transformation leads around the country looking for the new handbook for the new roles of social workers, but these new roles and the learning that supports them must be built with the people in the personal (and to a lesser extent, the community) circles. It is at this point, when it is important to remember that shift we discussed at the beginning of the chapter.

In terms of workforce, or learning and development, this translates into individuals being equal partners, both in learning and providing expertise, and crucially requires

those of us who have been responsible for commissioning learning and qualifications to be able to respond in a more individual and flexible way to what people say is important for them.

We have been working with local authority and PCT members of Inclusion North to begin to understand what the new professional roles will be by understanding what the best outcome would be from the perspectives of people in the personal circle first. Only when we hold that in mind, can we begin to understand how roles need to change.

In our opinion, this requires a true understanding of what it means to be a learning organisation (Senge, 1990). While local authorities are learning what the new roles need to look like so that they can provide the best results for people's lives, it's important that they are supported to be reflective and understanding of what they are discovering. At The Really Useful Learning Company, we call this approach 'The Learning Wheel' and it can be used with providers and local authorities to implement personalisation, and learn and produce training as part of one continuous process.

Be wary of anyone who thinks they have all the answers when it comes to the learning and new roles required for personalisation to work well in people's lives.

The professional circle goes on to include personal assistants (PAs). There has been some interesting debate (Brindle, 2008) about the rights of PAs to be a recognised, possibly registered profession. The Skills for Care and GSCC research the article refers to (Skills for Care, 2008a), interviewed over 500 people who use direct payments face to face, but excluded the individual budget pilot sites. Findings led the GSCC to announce a consultation on the development of a register for personal assistants, which potentially has significant repercussions for the workforce development of a personal assistant register.

When asked about possible regulation of the personal assistant workforce, the majority of direct payment employers felt that an official list of registered workers to assist them in recruitment would be useful and nine out of 10 personal assistants thought that registration was a good idea. However, there were mixed views among direct payment employers about whether such a system should be enforced. In contrast, the majority of personal assistants thought that registration should be introduced on a compulsory basis.

However, and despite the GSCC's reassurances that any register would have to fit with the new freedoms made available to people (GSCC, 2008), it raises some concerns. The research does not take account of the different workforce profile that emerges when the person receives their direct payment under the model of individual budgets,

and the flexibility and creativity that is supported in this system. Many more people make use of a blend of technical support, natural (or unpaid) support, and a new sort of PA. Many of these PAs are not what you would consider part of the traditional PA workforce and don't consider themselves to be part of a wider social care workforce, but come directly from a special area of interest the person has. Take the example of Ben in Essex who has a learning disability. He has two PAs to support him, one of whom has a background in social care, the other owns a recording studio. Ben, as a rapper, found someone from the community circle who can support him, and he does so, not only with his music, but in other areas of his life as well.

Any compulsory registration of all PAs would severely limit the flexibility that people currently have to blend their support across the three circles. It would impact on the availability of funds for individualised training and direct focus and attention to a national minimum standard rather than the best for each individual concerned.

However, it is essential that PAs and their employers have access to affordable, excellent learning that best supports them to make a positive difference in the life of the person they support, which should predominantly be agreed on an individual basis. (see **figure 2**). Just as individual budgets have started to unlock social care money, so we must continue this unlocking of resources and ensure that workforce development money begins to appear more consistently in people's individual budget and that they are considered well placed to make best use of it.

It is important to ask what impact nationally imposed professional qualifications for PAs have on the life of an individual who is being supported. It takes considerable financial investment on the part of the sector skills council, providers and sometimes the learner themselves to achieve these mandatory qualifications. And yet no attempt seems to have been made to measure the actual impact of these requirements on the quality of life of the people needing social care support.

We seem to assume that the greater the number of people who have a tested, measurable qualification, then the better the quality of life of the person they support. We suggest that these qualifications are ways of making society feel safe and secure, that society has somehow discharged its responsibility and the workforce is competent and 'safe'.

We recognise that there are people and families who value a clearly regulated set of qualifications to which they can refer workers. And we also recognise the right of all people and their families to choose the learning that is right for them and their learners (whether statutory or not). We are not assuming that the existing formal qualifications bring no value to either the individual or the learner.

However, we recognise the inherent limitations of nationally imposed regulations. They can never hope to meet the specific needs of each individual who uses the social care system. If we rely solely on nationally imposed regulations, we will at best create a lowest common denominator approach to learning for social care, at worst a set of qualifications that ticks boxes on a CV rather than providing learning that makes a really positive impact on the life of an individual.

Tools and tips

The balanced learning model

The balanced learning model is a tool that can be used as a starting point to develop someone's learning plan. It can be used for people in PA roles as well as support workers in services, but where people support more than one individual, their learning plan would need to reflect what's important to and for each person they support.

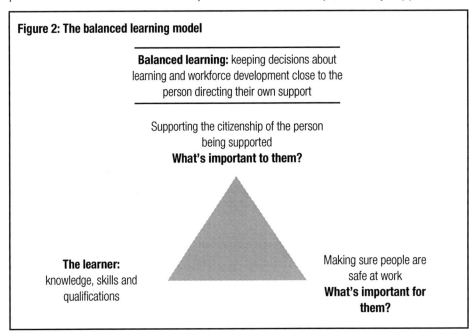

Figure 2: The balanced learning model

Balanced learning: keeping decisions about learning and workforce development close to the person directing their own support

Supporting the citizenship of the person being supported
What's important to them?

The learner: knowledge, skills and qualifications

Making sure people are safe at work
What's important for them?

This model ensures that choices in learning balance the needs of the learner with the rights of the person being supported, and learning that is required to keep people safe at work. This would also result in a more open market where the qualifications are undertaken when they have a demonstrable impact on the life of the person being supported and are of benefit to the continued professional development of the learner. This should have a positive impact on the quality of training providers and qualifications themselves.

Personalisation: Practical thoughts and ideas from people making it happen   © OLM-Pavilion 2009

What is important to do?

We must be prepared to consider requirements arising from an individual's plan in a creative and innovative way, so that we are ready to consider requirements that fall outside of the traditional learning and development arena, as well as more traditional, predictable requirements.

For example, imagine an individual who wants to work. Driving is out of the question for this person and they live in a rural community where public transport is severely limiting their access to work. They have chosen to employ a person to support them because of that person's approach and the integrity of their relationship. But the employed learner can't drive. For that individual, it may be relevant and important to financially support the learner with driving lessons.

This is radically different to the traditional approach to workforce learning. If we accept that the purpose of the learner in that individual's life is to primarily make a positive difference in that person's life, we must accept that the most relevant learning for that learner may be driving lessons.

Equally, and more traditionally, there are some obvious areas that an individual will want their learners to have skills in, for example, awareness around certain health conditions.

The knowledge, skills and qualifications of the worker

Understanding what learning someone needs is inextricably linked to their existing knowledge, skills and qualifications. A balanced learning approach to the learner's plan will help the learner identify what they already know, leading them to begin to identify the gaps in their knowledge and understanding.

Taking care to properly take account of what the learner is bringing to the plan will impact on how the learner views the relevance of the plan and how much ownership they will feel over it. It is dispiriting to develop a new plan with each new job. The balanced learning plan should be the start of a plan that the learner takes with him/herself wherever their career takes them.

What is important for someone?

The 'important for' part of the balanced learning model should be what's needed to keep the person being supported, and the person providing the support, safe and well. We must only produce minimum statutory learning that includes whatever is needed to keep people safe at work. Meeting the introduction for national minimum standards for support workers has typically absorbed much of the training budget of most providers, leaving them unable to fund the learning that would arguably make the most difference to the lives of the individuals being supported.

Principles of workforce redesign

These principles for workforce redesign (Skills for Care, 2008b) provide some useful ways of approaching large-scale workforce redesign.

The seven principles of workforce redesign set out the key things you need to take account of when changing the way in which your staff work to meet the challenges of the personalisation agenda. They are an important framework for workforce reform and will be refined and supported by other tools.

1. Take a whole systems view of organisational change

- By understanding how people relate to each other in organisations and across partnerships, you are more likely to know what needs to change.
- Remember that staff, people who use services and carers (ie. family or friends) are all part of this system and cannot be treated in isolation from it.
- A planning and workforce development process that is participatory, inclusive and evolving has more chance of success.
- Be aware that the culture and the character of an organisation or partnership is determined by the people who work for it and who typically take responsibility for problems and solutions.
- Make supporting people in different parts of the system through the whole process of change integral to your strategy and vision.

2. Recognise how people, organisations and partnerships respond differently to change

- Make sure that you remember that change can be threatening to individuals, making them feel 'deskilled' and vulnerable. People are particularly resistant to change that goes against the current work culture.
- Ensure that resources to support change are in place.
- People learn and change at different rates, so change programmes need to be flexible enough to accommodate this.
- Opportunities need to be available to support individuals in developing the skills and expertise they need to work in redesigned services.

3. Nurture champions, innovators and leaders

- If you create an environment in which managed risk is acceptable, people will feel safe to experiment.
- Make sure you seek out those individuals who are champions, innovators and leaders – support and sustain them by encouraging them to share their learning, including failures.

Personalisation: Practical thoughts and ideas from people making it happen   © OLM-Pavilion 2009

■ Provide high quality supervision and you will empower people to be innovative, dynamic, adaptable and flexible.

4. Engage people in the process – acknowledge and value their experience

■ Recognise the value of people to organisations and partnerships. Encourage the use of life experience in the workplace, and seek out the learning from the work that people are involved in.

■ Learn what works in practice from those people directly involved in it. Create systems and processes that encourage the sharing of learning across organisations and partnerships.

■ Encourage the contributions of all (not just managers) in creating an environment that is a good place to work. Share learning across the organisation and partnerships – using people's learning and experience to support service transformation.

5. Be aware of the ways adults learn

■ Understand that adults are goal-oriented, and need to see the benefits of any learning they are required to undertake.

■ Remember that adults are keen to learn where they see a practical application and can use their learning to help them solve problems.

■ In learning, the process of how the learning takes place can be as important as the content.

6. Change minds and change systems

■ Change attitudes and behaviour in order to ensure long-lasting success. As people develop new attitudes and behaviours they are better able to contribute to the organisation and partnership goals.

■ Encourage experimentation, listen to people's experiences, encourage questioning, and utilise the experience and learning of individuals in the process of workforce redesign.

■ Never be satisfied with only 'doing the same better'; continually reflect on what you deliver to fundamentally improve the quality of your services.

7. Develop workforce strategies that support transformation and recognise the shape of resources available in the local community

- Understand the people that make up your local community, acknowledge how they like to work and live and make the work and resources you have on offer attractive to them.
- Recognise that the people living in the local community who require support services will increasingly require a wider choice of services from which to choose. This will require people to broaden the range of skills they have.
- Build links across traditional boundaries to support the transformation of services.

Case studies – personal stories

J, a parent in Bristol

A's ELP (essential lifestyle plan – a person-centred plan) drives his service so it makes sense that the ELP identifies the training that people need. As recipients of a direct payment we are able to access statutory training from our local authority. To date, everyone has received the safeguarding vulnerable adults training, which is good, but we need something that's slightly different, there are additional vulnerabilities for those in individualised services. The training department have agreed to provide some bespoke in-house training.

Everyone gets first aid training and we are soon to get all staff onto epilepsy awareness training because A has recently developed epilepsy.

We buy positive response training and any additional training needs that become apparent during regular supervisions are sourced. All staff receive certification for training completed, which makes up their personal portfolios. One of A's best support workers is a man who really struggles with written English. It would be awful if he had to do formal learning like an NVQ because we would lose him, and A would lose one of his best support workers.

We don't want to recruit academics to support A, we want to recruit people who love life, who have lots of energy and who understand the importance of person-centred practice. We're talking about people, not qualifications.

D, individual budget user, Essex

When I lived in Primrose Grove (supported living house) the staff used to go off on training courses. I never knew what the training was that they did. None of them ever took time to explain what they were learning, and no one ever asked me if I thought it was the right training.

Personalisation: Practical thoughts and ideas from people making it happen   © OLM-Pavilion 2009

I didn't get the right support in that place. Now I live in my own place and I am married. My wife and I support each other now and we have a baby on the way. I will want support from support staff, and I know what skills I want them to have. I want someone who will support me to be a good parent, to help me support my baby to develop as a person. I want to be able to decide what training is important for my support staff.

> **Note:** The two stories that follow are transcripts of an interview conducted as part of a Department of Health project, Choice and Control.

V, D's sister, Worcester

The D that lived for nearly 30 years in residential care was a really disruptive, challenging and difficult individual and I wouldn't have said anything different myself. She had so many labels on her there just wasn't any spare room and every review, everywhere she went it was always that she was one of the most difficult people in the house that she was being supported in. She took lots of care, she took lots of hard work and she was difficult to manage. She was disruptive, she was argumentative, she was crying and screeching all the time, and nothing was very pleasant for her or the people working with her. But it was all about the not understanding her and she couldn't communicate, she had no voice, so she had no say, and the only way she could demonstrate she was frustrated or unhappy was by throwing a shoe or slamming doors or screaming at other people, all those kinds of things. And her behaviour was so extreme that you would never have ever imagined that she could live independently as she's doing now.

I was told from the very beginning, even by her own social worker, for two reasons that she'd never live alone: 1) cost – there's no way, you'll have to buddy her up with certain people and 2) she's someone with severe and complex needs. But we didn't have anything to lose. Things were not good where she lived before, so it was worth trying something different. And I just had the imagination and thought that if it doesn't work, what have we lost? So let's go for it, let's try. And from the very beginning I knew that D could do these things and I think I was the only one who did believe, even the GP was sort of saying, 'This can't be. D couldn't cope in this way'. And literally from the very first day she came into her own environment, with her own staff, we've had a better, calmer person. It didn't take long, I mean the improvement was immense from the days, then weeks, then months. We've got someone now who is showing her own natural intelligence in so many ways and showing that she can run her own house.

Yes, what we decided was that the induction would be as long or as slow a process as need be really. Each person was very, very individual and it was about D getting to know them. D, from the minute she moved into this house felt at home. She felt it

was her residence, she was in charge and she made that categorically clear from the beginning.

What mattered most of all was just getting to know D, just getting to make sure the people felt comfortable with her and she felt comfortable with them. Because she's quite a robust person, she's like having a tornado coming in and out of the house, bang and there's sometimes quite a lot of noise and clutter and she's a very, very busy person, and people had to get to identify with all of that and understand that is just D's way, and how she is as a person and there's no point trying to change her.

But for me to understand D's lifestyle, to understand about D's condition, you know, about autism was very, very important. It's quite specialised, it's quite expensive and as yet I have had trouble finding, well I haven't had the funds. I haven't had the money. So who would help us with that? That's an area where I've had a lot of promise, but no feedback or actual happening other than small things we've been doing for ourselves.

So to me, whoever's got an individual budget and whatever they need to make life better for them and their staff, training's a very important part of it and should be there to let people develop in whatever way they want.

J, mum to M, personal health budget holder, Blackburn

Q. Why did you write an induction specific to M?

Because, and this was highlighted by our experience of the training staff got through the hospital, this was one of the main drivers for us to get a personal budget, so that we could personalise the training. It seemed to me that some of the training they'd received in the past wasn't a very good fit. There would be sort of some of the underpinning knowledge but to me it's the translating into practice that's the most important part. So although you might understand how to do something, because M doesn't follow the rules in textbooks, what's really important to us is that the way things are done are right for him.

There's also the issue for people with life limiting conditions. M has a life limiting condition so if something happens to him, we want to make sure that our staff are skilled and equipped to enter the workforce and support somebody else, that's really important to us.

Q. How do you fund the training?

We have an element in the budget that's for training. It's not a substantial amount, in fact it's probably not adequate. What we've done so far is been as

resourceful as we can in getting free training. Fortunately the three people who wanted to do their NVQ 3 were eligible for Skills for Care money so we're not having to pay for that, which is really important. The PCT has recognised that there is a new market out there, there will be more families required to provide mandatory training and they've allowed our staff to use their resource to use their training so we've used their manual handling and first aid.

We were offered some moving and handling training through the council and there's a sense that it ticks the box, but there was a lot of the content that was not relevant and not helpful in this setting. What would have been really useful is if the trainer had come to our home to actually train on our equipment, on our ceiling track hoist, on our mobile hoist and get a better sense of what the difficulties are around moving and handling, especially as M approached adulthood and is quite big now. And also there are all sorts of complications like what do I do with M's vent when I'm moving him at night to change him, do I have to take it off? There are all sorts of complications, so if we'd had someone training in-house, that would have been much more useful.

So for us, it's been about being as resourceful as we can but there has been some training we haven't been able to access because it's so expensive.

References

Brindle D (2008) Does personalisation of care and support services inevitably mean casualisation of the workforce? *The Guardian,* 2 July.

Duffy S (2006) *Keys to Citizenship*: *A guide to getting good support services for people with learning difficulties* (2nd ed). Birkenhead: Paradigm Consultancy and Development Agency.

Glendinning C, Challis D, Fernández J-L, Jacobs S, Jones K, Knapp M, Manthorpe J, Moran N, Netten A, Stevens M & Wilberforce M (2008) Evaluation of the Individual Budgets Pilot Programme: Final report. York: Social Policy Research Unit.

GSCC (2008) *Consultation Announced on the Regulation of Personal Assistants*, Press release 30 June. London: GSCC.

Needham C & Carr S (2009) *Research Briefing 31: Co-production, an emerging evidence base for adult social care.* London: SCIE.

Poll C & Duffy S (2008) *A Report on In Control's Second Phase.* London: In Control.

Senge P (1990) *The Fifth Discipline: The art and practice of the learning organisation.* New York: Random House.

Skills for Care (2008a) *The Employment Aspects and Workforce Implications of Direct Payments.* London: Skills for Care.

Skills for Care (2008b) *The Principles of Workforce Redesign: A framework for service transformation in adult social care* [online]. Leeds: Skills for Care. Available at: www.skillsforcare.org.uk/research/new_types_of_worker/Principlesredesign.aspx (accessed August 2009).

Chapter 11

Rebel with a cause

Sarah Wood

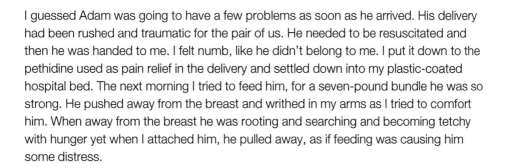

I guessed Adam was going to have a few problems as soon as he arrived. His delivery had been rushed and traumatic for the pair of us. He needed to be resuscitated and then he was handed to me. I felt numb, like he didn't belong to me. I put it down to the pethidine used as pain relief in the delivery and settled down into my plastic-coated hospital bed. The next morning I tried to feed him, for a seven-pound bundle he was so strong. He pushed away from the breast and writhed in my arms as I tried to comfort him. When away from the breast he was rooting and searching and becoming tetchy with hunger yet when I attached him, he pulled away, as if feeding was causing him some distress.

We took him home to his big sister, Cori, then 21 months old. He had a poor swallow, thus most feeds ended up with him purple in the face, coughing, crying and with me ending up feeling, quite frankly, a little worse than useless. My house was a mess, having recently moved into a place that needed a total refurbishment. My daughter was beginning to display the typical signs of jealousy at the new arrival. My husband was not particularly supportive; frequently losing his patience with Adam's crying and Cori's age appropriate behaviour. I had a massive post-delivery haemorrhage and before long, after struggling with my own ill health, a toddler and a poorly baby, I sank into a pit of postnatal depression. My already fragile marriage dissolved before Adam was two years old.

From that moment on, none of my anxieties about my baby seemed to be listened to. Now I had the label of 'over anxious mum' on top of everything else.

The first year of Adam's life was a flurry of laundry, playgroup, housework, feeding, bathing, shopping and generally trying to hold it all together. While at the same time, Adam seemed not to notice or care if I was there or not. I had huge problems weaning him, still pureeing food at a year old. He refused to put anything to his mouth, like most babies do. He had seemingly constant chest infections. Each visit to the family doctor

resulted in me feeling over protective or with a prescription for yet another course of antibiotics for Adam.

It was only when he failed his 15-month check that any of my concerns were taken seriously. The health visitor recommended that he be seen by a paediatrician. He was making no verbal sounds, he did not point at things, he seemed deaf, he could not feed properly, he was always vomiting, and he woke up frequently during the night struggling for breath. He seemed totally disinterested in the world around him. Yet he would sit happily for hours, spinning a single wheel on a toy car.

The paediatric appointment led to either us attending appointments or people visiting us at home. We saw a clinical psychologist, a psychiatrist, a learning disability nurse, a preschool teacher, a speech therapist, a physiotherapist, a play therapist, a family centre, a dietician, an ear, nose, throat (ENT) surgeon, a genetic counsellor, and an educational psychologist. Although all these appointments and visitors were a massive intrusion into an already busy and stressful time, I held out hope with each and every one. I hoped that the therapist would have Adam speaking. I was secure in the knowledge that the paediatrician would come up with a diagnosis that I could research and understand. I hoped I would find families in the same position and become an expert on my son's condition. I hoped that the ENT surgeon's suggestion of removing Adam's tonsils and adenoids and insertion of grommets would result in a healthy little boy who would miraculously begin eating a variety of foods instead of the bland puree that he seemed to prefer. I thought the psychologist would give me insight into his bizarre behaviours and help me to understand the weird rituals that were starting to become a huge part of our daily functioning. In short, I was desperate and truly grateful for anything the professionals could offer us.

A huge string of tests then began, assessments of this that and the other and I soon lost count of the number of times I was asked to describe his development. At what age did he smile at me? At what age did he first pull himself up? Did he turn his head if someone knocked at the front door? If so, how old was he when he first did this? It went on and on. In fact, it went on for years.

The paediatrician said to me when Adam was about seven years old, 'We usually just see kids like Adam once a year, to check there are no major health issues'. I remember that day, leaving the child development centre and feeling abandoned – years of appointments and meetings – for what?

I then spent years fighting for everything. I fought for a diagnosis (which was a battle not won until Adam was 19). I fought for nappies beyond the age of infancy (anyone having been subjected to a continence assessment will have full empathy for that

appointment!). I fought for a school place in our local language unit (and lost). I fought for respite so my daughter could have some normality in her life. I fought for speech and language therapy. I fought for meaningful activities for Adam. I fought for all the disability related benefits, Carers Allowance, Disability Living Allowance, the offer of a free washing machine, the occasional organised day trip and the provision of a wheelchair.

The thing that I never really questioned was the fact that all these battles ended in either losing or winning something that did not actually enhance our life. I was always frightened of complaining and suggesting things that would really help, like a bit of help with the cleaning or an extra pair of hands to make family outings a reality.

He was placed in expensive respite, which he found distressing, he was taken everywhere by mini bus or taxi. He was visited by lovely women who turned up wearing tabards, to take him out for a toasted teacake. He was **managed** and what we received in the way of services helped us to manage and cope. Nothing really fitted with our family routine or our personalities. Nothing actually made our lives any happier.

Like most families managing on social security benefits and the goodwill of decision makers, we became defensive and were constantly encouraged to describe the worst day, to justify what we were receiving for fear of it being taken away. This led to me only ever being able to see or describe Adam in the worst possible light. We constantly focused on the negativity of his condition. Not once did anyone ask me about Adam's passions, gifts, interests or strengths. Not once did anyone ask me about my own.

There was nothing in the way of support for his older sister who was beginning to see life for herself in disability world. When the other mums and kids got together for play and coffee times, Cori was invited but Adam and I had to stay at home. When other mums did their stint of playgroup duty, Adam and I had to stay at home. By the age of two, Adam had started to become excluded. He was a boisterous, noisy and sometimes destructive presence. He was incontinent and continued to be so for many years to come. He had severe asthma and needed a nebuliser frequently. Cori's playmates started declining the offer to come and have tea at our house. Other mums were too nervous to have him round to play in case he hurt smaller children, or in case he became upset or wanted something and they didn't know how to work out what he was saying. What they didn't know was that I knew none of these things either; Adam was a mystery to me too. I yearned to spend a day inside his head so I could help him or at least understand why he did the things he did.

It got to the point that when the kids went to bed at night I thanked God and congratulated myself on surviving another day. Life was pretty grim. And little did we know it was about to become even more so.

When Adam was 11 and was settled into his special school, I went to university for three years to undertake nurse training. It was in my second year that disaster struck. Our house had a fire and we had to move out. Due to problems with the builders we ended up being out of our own home for over four years. During this time we lived in a cramped and totally unsuitable house. We had belongings everywhere and boxes piled high. Many of our familiar items were in storage and this all had a massive negative impact on Adam, resulting in behaviour and sleep disturbances.

We continued life as best as we could and I did well at university despite becoming weak and exhausted, which I put down to studying long hours, working shifts at the hospital and caring for Adam.

We took the decision in 2004 to remove Adam from his respite facility because it was actually causing him more distress than staying at home and I could not handle the added pressure of the problems we faced before and after he went. The building was beautiful and the staff were great and hard working, but it was just not suitable for Adam. We were now managing alone. We were told around this time that Adam was to have a new care manager as he was now in 'transition'. We waited to see what new services were open to us as he headed into his teenage years.

I qualified as a staff nurse in 2004 and started work on a busy acute medical ward for the elderly. I was still feeling run down and had started losing a lot of weight. When my temperature started soaring to over 38 degrees for no apparent reason and my legs were black and blue with uncaused bruising, a doctor and colleague advised that I should have a blood test. I was devastated to find out a few weeks later that I had developed a rare form of leukaemia, which meant I needed to have six months chemotherapy.

This left me with a massive problem. Who was going to help with Adam? I needed to be at hospital for a whole day every two weeks and the few days after treatment were a blur of sore throats, vomiting, mouth ulcers, hair loss, wig fitting and fatigue that was the worst I have ever known. On top of this, I would cry myself to sleep every night as I tried to imagine Adam in the world without me. Who would understand him? Who would ensure he had what he wanted and needed? Who would take the time to get to know him and make efforts to make sure his future was good and happy? My fear of death and dying became focused so much on my fear of leaving Adam behind that I hardly thought about the process from my own point of view. I wasn't busy telling friends which hymns I would like or choosing my favourite flowers, I was panicking about my son and I have never before or since known a fear like it. I did not trust the world enough to look out for him.

Personalisation: Practical thoughts and ideas from people making it happen   © OLM-Pavilion 2009

A wonderful woman who used to also be a nurse at our local hospital, and her husband, offered to take Adam after school on chemotherapy days and keep him overnight. I asked our care manager to fast track her through the Sharing Care scheme, approval process. She could now be paid for her help. It made it a lot easier for me to accept her offer with a clean conscience once I knew she was being remunerated. Adam already knew this delightful couple and was more than happy to go and stay with them every fortnight. For the first time, since Adam was born, I felt that someone was on our side and I felt a little less alone.

Adam has a passion for cars and keeping them clean and tidy. He spent hours with my friend's husband washing his car and looking at cars on the internet and helping him with his car maintenance. Whenever Adam went to stay with his new friends, he was enthusiastic and eager to leave us. This is priceless, it meant I could truly relax and hardly give him another thought while he was away. I could concentrate on getting better and sleep peacefully, rather than waiting for the telephone to ring for him to be brought home, or feeling guilty knowing he was terribly unhappy.

I didn't realise it at the time, but we had actually started our journey of self-directed support. At Adam's annual review the care managers celebrated the link between Adam and his sharing carers, but I remember thinking, 'We did it, not you! We found the right people, not you. We made it happen, not you'.

In the time off work after my treatment had finished, I was invited to attend a five-day course about planning with people. I had a vague idea about person-centred planning as I had recently completed an assignment about it as part of my nurse training, but had no idea how to make it happen for Adam. The course really did change our lives. We were talked through the planning process, looking particularly at PATH and MAP planning tools. We learned how to facilitate these meetings for people and how to uncover seeds of dreams and how to identify gifts, talents and passions of people rather than just caring for them.

I went home and tried a little bit of what I had learned with Adam. I played some relaxing music and got our pens and paper out. I asked him to draw a picture. He spent a long time drawing a picture of two boys in a school classroom. One of the boys was dressed from head to toe in blue. 'Who's this?' I asked. 'It's Pete.' 'Why is he in blue?' 'It's his favourite colour.' 'Why have you drawn Pete?' 'He's my friend.' 'But Pete is older than you, he has left your school now.' 'I know.' 'Do you want to see more of Pete?' 'Yes.' 'Shall I ring Pete's mum and try and sort something out for him to come for tea one night?' 'Yes please.'

I had not realised that Pete and his friendship had meant so much to Adam. It was a massive insight to discover that just because Adam did not have the skills to maintain a friendship, this did not mean that he did not want or need a friendship. From that day on we have kept regular contact with Pete and his parents. Pete and Adam enjoy a fulfilling and longstanding friendship. They have been on holiday together, socialised together, shared personal assistants and are hoping to live together in the future.

This took about half-an-hour to find out and only a telephone call to make happen. All I had done was learn, after 14 years, to listen.

We then went on and organised a PATH meeting. I invited mainly friends of my own as Adam's circle of friends was still very small. We had a great day and it was fantastic to hear all the positive things that people had noticed over the years about Adam, things I had not known.

Instead of 'obsessive' he became 'neat and tidy', instead of 'painfully shy' or 'mute', he became 'quiet and conscientious', instead of being 'repetitive and boring' he became 'brilliant at retaining factual knowledge'. It was wonderful to hear him being described in positive ways, to see his life being looked at in a hopeful way, to see people giving him ideas on how his future could look and all the brilliant things he can do, achieve, and become. All his choices and aspirations came out, all his hopes and dreams were looked at, celebrated and encouraged. I felt as though, even if I dropped down dead after that meeting, he would have a whole load of people looking out for him, making sure he was listened to and understood. I no longer saw a picture of him with a dead mum and no one to care.

We started the ball rolling by looking at him getting out and about. He was allowed three hours a week of direct payments. One of my daughter's friends became his personal assistant, she also happened to be a model. So Adam's first outing to the pub to play pool was with a model. It's a story I love to tell. From being transported around in a taxi to somewhere he did not want to go, to going out on the bus for an orange juice and a good night on the town with a gorgeous stunner! Life was starting to look brighter.

Adam desperately wanted to go everywhere under his own steam by cycling. We were not aware of this until he drew a tiny little picture of a bike on his PATH plan. This led to further exploration; a dream of getting himself to school each morning, instead of being picked up in a taxi, emerged. We decided to make it happen. His school was about seven miles from home and meant journeying right through the city centre, not a journey I would be prepared to undertake. We enlisted the help of the independent travel co-ordinator. He helped Adam find a safe (but a lot longer) route to school.

Adam has always despised public transport but was persuaded by the travel trainer to 'give the bus a go'. 'There may be a time when you have something heavy to carry. Or the weather may be terrible one day.'

Adam agreed and training commenced in the use of the bus. Adam was unwilling to speak verbally to the driver but once we got him a pass that he could just hold up as he boarded, he was away. He even studied the bus route and timetable to such a degree that one day, without my knowledge or permission, he went around the whole route twice before getting to school, he left the house at 6am, waving as he drove past my shocked face one morning as I made my way back from the 24-hour garage with the morning milk.

When it came to Adam's annual review, we had previously been seated in his headmaster's office around a table with various people, some who we knew and some who we had never met before. The chairperson was often someone who had not previously been introduced to us or Adam. We decided (as a result of reading the *Valuing People* white paper) that Adam should have a review in which he was represented as the person he is and who he wants to be seen as. Historically, Adam had found his annual review to be a traumatic event. After one in particular, he said he had to nip his bottom as he said, 'I was going to poo myself with fear'.

We made Adam's next review accessible to him. We insisted it was held in a place and in a style that Adam was comfortable with. So from then on, Adam's reviews followed a set of guidelines that he had decided upon. No one was to wear a suit, the review had to take place in Adam's home, we had Christmas carols playing in the background despite it being July, we graphically recorded the meeting in bright colours on a huge paper table cover, we had balloons that were patted back and forth between people, we had sweets and individual cartons of juice instead of the teas and coffees that were usually offered. Adam spoke up at these meetings and some care staff, who had been involved with Adam for years, heard him speak for the first time.

We then moved on to employing a personal assistant for 10 hours a week. This meant Adam could have whole day trips and get out and about even more. We employed a friend of the family who is the same age as Adam. Cori and I had a couple of proper nights out during this time. We went out drinking, dancing and had no need to rush home because Adam was at home, staying up late with a mate, having pizza and playing on his games console. Our life was beginning to take the shape of something we had not experienced for a long time – something called choice and normality. We saved some hours up and took the personal assistant on holiday with us. This was the first successful family holiday we had in 17 years.

We moved on to a full individualised budget last year. Initially we used some of the money to buy a hot tub for our back yard. When Adam sits in the warm water at the end of each day, he becomes relaxed and communicates well. He then sleeps right through the night, which was something that was also new to us – eight hours, straight through. After 17 years of interrupted sleep, believe me, it was money well spent.

Instead of taking up the offer of a residential, out-of-county placement when Adam left school, we decided to use Adam's budget to employ a personal assistant for 32 hours a week. Adam now has a day each week when he buys his own food and toiletries. He changes his own bed, he pre-cooks some of his own meals for the week ahead. He works one day a week valeting the cars of our local learning disability staff team, he attends a gym, he cycles regularly, long distance, which in turn keeps him fit, relaxed and known to the neighbourhood.

It came up in one of Adam's friendship meetings that he loves listening to stories from the past. So we thought about all the elderly people who live in isolation, who would be happy to spend some time each week chatting to Adam. He became a regular visitor to an elderly gentleman who lived up our street and this continued after the gentleman was admitted to residential care.

The individual budget allows me to pay for some domestic help, which frees me up to oversee the planning and organising of his budget and also makes the day-to-day, full-time personal care of Adam a lot easier.

In the future we plan to help Adam secure his own home and live with whomever he chooses and be supported by people he can trust and who have his absolute best interest at heart.

Although the individual budget has helped immensely (albeit a fraction of the cost of the unsuitable services) I have to add that most of the changes that directly benefit Adam and our family are the changes in the way we think. I had to be taught (I am ashamed to say) to see Adam as a citizen and a true member of our community, so it's hardly any wonder that others did not see him positively. Our neighbours used to see Adam getting picked up in mini buses or taxis and taken to mysterious places. Now they see him waiting at the bus stop, going out on his bike, washing cars on the garage forecourt, using our local shops and visiting his mates.

It's taken many years and lots of hard work. The gaps in the system put an awful lot of pressure on family members. We are all still learning and we have a long way to go. For Adam, his life has changed beyond all recognition. He determines himself, his day

and his future with the support of those he loves and trusts. For me, I no longer have a deep-seated fear of leaving him alone in the world, so I can get on and live my life too.

Adam finally got a diagnosis last year of autism, but it hardly seems important now. Adam is Adam. He is who he is. He's my son and I am so proud of the way he lives his life. I have had many challenges over the years but when I see the challenges Adam faces every day it makes me so proud to call myself his mum.

Adam was consistently and maliciously bullied while using the bus. A group of boys were reported as spitting on him and laughing at him, before photographing him on their mobile phones and sharing the joke. This went on for weeks until a member of the public made someone aware. Adam had not complained or let anyone know that this was happening. His autism makes it difficult for him to share anything, including information. My gut instinct was keep him safe by returning to taxis for his transport. 'No way!' he laughed when I suggested this to him. 'But then you won't have to worry about the boys spitting on you again,' I offered, trying to achieve some peace of mind. 'I don't want taxis. I love my life now.' And the next day he was back out there waiting for his bus.

I have often heard carers say that they want just a 'little bit of life' of their own. I have met mums who have never managed to read a book or who have lost touch socially due to the restraints of being a carer. Self-directed support can mean an end to that. Families can take the opportunity to exercise control over their lives, as we have done with ours.

At best, in the past, people who have met me and know my story tended to feel sorry for me. I was waving a friend off the other day and she shouted, 'See ya.' I replied, 'Wouldn't want to be ya'.

She got in her car and shouted back, 'Yeah but I wouldn't mind being YOU!' For someone to feel envious of our life was unimaginable a few years ago. Through making our own decisions we cannot only say that we now 'have a life' but that we have, at last, created a great one.

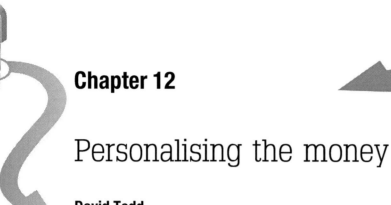

Chapter 12

Personalising the money

David Todd

Introduction

We were sitting in a café one Friday afternoon, having a coffee, celebrating the culmination of nine months of hard work – myself, the project lead and the social worker. The first service user, in the borough, had been paid their first instalment of their personal budget. Personal budget, individual budget, direct payment, we agreed it didn't matter what we called it – this citizen had been given the opportunity to take control and make choices about how to manage the delivery of services to meet their needs. We were really happy, but tired – to get to the start line had been hard work.

From the first time I heard about self-directed support (my preferred label) I knew this wouldn't be easy – but I knew the results would be worth it. In this short piece I'll cover some of my experiences with self-directed support and aim to illustrate that with good, committed people around you, things can happen and even the biggest, oldest ships can be turned at least a few degrees towards a better future – particularly if you use a very different way of dealing with money as a way of giving the rudder a big push.

I begin with how I got involved in self-directed support and how the elegance, simplicity and benefits of the approach captured my attention. Then I will move onto some of the detailed work I have supported, and finally I summarise the key challenges that I see are ahead of us.

How self-directed support found me

I am a director of a small consulting company. We are committed to improving public services. I always knew I wouldn't make a good nurse or social worker, even so, I wanted to make a small contribution and have focused on supporting public sector organisations to improve the way the public system functions and ensure we all get value for money.

In 2005 I was working with a local authority whose financial position, to say the least, was unfavourable. An element of the work was to review a number of options and assess the impact they could have on the financial situation currently being felt and the predicted future position, which also didn't look terribly favourable. One of the options we discussed and tested was self-directed support.

Through discussion, debate and analysis it was shown that self-directed support was financially sound and based on the results of pilots in other local authorities – a good idea that represented a real opportunity for citizens.

Once it was agreed that self-directed support should be explored, a pilot project was established. Since then I have worked with numerous local authorities on a range of issues in relation to self-directed support. One of the main areas has been the development and implementation of resource allocation systems (RAS), this chapter describes some of my experience and some of the things I have noticed.

Development resource allocation systems

The RAS is more than it seems

The RAS is often the starting point for local authorities beginning the journey towards self-directed support. This is understandable – it is a very tangible task and contains the key components of assessment, care management and finance that always get peoples' attention. With all of this, I have found that most RASs take a lot longer to develop than originally planned. Why is this?

Simple, what often gets missed is the fact that by being one of the first elements that local authorities decide to tackle, it takes on a broader role. With the RAS being people's first taste of self-directed support, means lots of questioning, lots of challenging and lots of discussion that needs to be navigated before, during and after developing the technical RAS solution. Having developed a number of resource allocation systems with local authorities, I strongly believe the technical task to be very doable and relatively straightforward. In contrast, managing the questions, expectations and fears of stakeholders is much more challenging.

Knowing this fact, it is even more surprising to see councils delegating this task to a finance person or an outside contractor, when a wider range of skills are needed, such as engaging with different stakeholders (for example staff, citizens, carers, providers, senior management), managing expectations and being able to maintain the context or vision of self-directed support while at the same time ensuring the technical RAS tasks are robust and delivered. From my experience, the best approaches have involved a group of people with technical as well as these 'softer' skills, with different people leading on different elements.

Personalisation: Practical thoughts and ideas from people making it happen   © OLM-Pavilion 2009

By understanding this wider role the RAS can be used to support detailed conversations about what self-directed support is aiming to achieve and be used to create the platform for building the understanding, transparency and learning required to make self-directed support function.

Simple and elegant is better

All a RAS has to do is translate personally identified needs into an indicative budget that helps fund the support plan. Simple and elegant, RASs are perfectly capable of enabling this.

- A RAS does not have to cover every possible area of need or personal situation but work for a population of service users with diverse needs, ambitions and desired outcomes.
- From experience, RASs that focus on large amounts of assessment and very detailed financial analysis tend not to accurately represent the functional needs of the service user and replicate historic patterns of expenditure. I thought we were aiming to move away from historical patterns of what has been shown a number of times to be inequitable patterns of expenditure. I also feel that the more technical RASs are, the more difficult they are to implement, to explain to service users and carers, and they don't create the context or environment needed to stimulate the innovation and creativity central to the success self-directed support.

Using a RAS with real people is the only way to learn

When developing and implementing RASs, discussions often take place exploring different situations, for example, what will we do if X or Y happens? The financial sustainability of a new RAS is a topic that is often discussed. While I do support a level of analysis into the financial sustainability of any RAS, I believe it is very difficult to gauge the sustainability of such a component of self-directed support when seen in isolation. The RAS is only one part of the bigger picture of self-directed support and cannot be analysed in isolation of the other components, which need to be put in place for a system of self-directed support to function appropriately. In addition, the RAS is attempting to create vastly different financial dynamics throughout the system, which will impact on sustainability.

Therefore, undertaking live usage and testing of a RAS model as early as possible is important. To ensure that local authorities extract the most value from the process, it is important to collect accurate data on the usage of the RAS, review this data and learn from this process in order to improve the RAS and other components of self-directed support.

My overall impression has been that some of the concerns that people have before implementing a RAS model in most cases do not eventuate. These concerns come from the old system and do not exist within a system of self-directed support.

Moving from pilot to a new way of working

About three years ago all (almost all) self-directed support work was in pilot phase. Pilots are great, there is lots of innovation, committed people, flexibility and often, due to a range of complex factors result in positive outputs demonstrating that the idea is something that should be rolled out more widely. Then why do the outputs from a full-scale implementation never seem to match those from a pilot?

Over the last 12 months or so, a number of local authorities have begun full-scale implementation of self-directed support across all care groups. While this is excellent and where all local authorities should be heading, it also presents a number of challenges. One of the major challenges I have seen is the desire to reign in the flexibility inherent in most pilots and begin to recreate levels of bureaucracy within the new system. This results in the creation of policies, forms, governance structures and processes. While some of this is necessary to upscale self-directed support, the risk is that the innovation and creativity evident in early pilots is lost and what we get is the same old system with slightly different wrapping paper.

Overall, I feel there is an overwhelming comfort in the current system – even though people accept that it doesn't really support people to have the lives they desire and is also expensive. It is known and understood and there are a number of people who are happier holding onto the current system than changing and having to learn something new.

One of the drivers reinforcing this situation is the performance requirements placed on local authorities. On one hand, managers are told to save money and create efficiencies and on the other they are told to take risks and innovate – at the same time meeting the same old performance measures. My experience with councils is that some feel very hamstrung by the performance culture and in some cases have had to actually go against various performance requirements to pilot and then implement self-directed support – something has to give.

Involving citizens and providers in designing the new system

Some local authorities involve citizens and providers really well – others do this very badly. I am not talking about representatives on partnership boards or advisory groups, I mean involving citizens and providers in the development of the system of self-directed support including the RAS. This means having them at the table and in some cases coming in for criticism.

Where citizens and providers have been involved in implementations, I can honestly say that the outputs have been of better quality and are more able to be implemented. It is also advantageous to have people who go back to their networks and talk about self-directed support – supporting the communication of what is happening and harnessing the innovating of the whole community.

Other things I have noticed developing RASs

- The biggest challenge is culture change.
- Engagement is key, so engage with stakeholders early. Involve as many people in the design of the new system. Do not worry if you have nothing tangible to offer people, starting the discussions and involving people in the design of solutions early creates buy-in.
- Run seminars and workshops early in the process to get people thinking about self-directed support. People will ask tough questions. These should be expected and if we want all people pulling in the same direction then we need better answers.

The challenges to come

- Stimulating and developing the market for self-directed support.
  - There are some councils leading the way on this front, however, most appear to be behind the eight ball. Shaping the market will take years, not months and requires action now.
  - Commissioning must be aligned with this agenda. I recently heard a story of a council, implementing self-directed support and realised that a number of people were choosing to use their personal budget on the same service. Commissioners heard about this and decided that if the council offered a block contract to the provider they could negotiate a discount. This goes totally against self-directed support and shows that the commissioners don't understand what self-directed support is aiming to achieve. Old style commissioning will not deliver the innovation required to make this work – we need better approaches and models.
- Understanding what citizens really want from self-directed support.
  - I only know of a few councils who are systematically collecting real time information on what citizens are spending their personal budgets on, and more importantly what they would spend it on if those things were available.
  - This information is important to all stakeholders so that commissioners can signal to the market where the gaps are, so brokers can support citizens to source alternatives and for providers to know where demand is heading.

■ Anticipating the impact of changes in performance criteria.

    ■ Self-directed support is going to make some good local authorities look worse and some not so good ones look better. How comfortable are some local authorities to weather the storm until they can demonstrate that this agenda really makes a difference to the lives of citizens? Hopefully long enough.

Final word

So looking back to the Friday afternoon in the café and being tired. Has it all been worth it? Yes. For me this work has been some of the most challenging but rewarding I have been involved in. I have had the pleasure of working with some extremely committed and passionate people who really are making a difference and helping people to take control.

Finally, I just heard that the young man who received that first payment has just started his first ever job at the local community centre. His mum says he is the happiest she has ever seen him and she has a new lease of life in her role as a carer – the hard work is definitely worth it.

Personalisation: Practical thoughts and ideas from people making it happen   © OLM-Pavilion 2009

Chapter 13

Co-production

Helen Sanderson, Tony Bennett and Sam Newman

Introduction

In 2008 the Department of Health commissioned two pieces of work that were to be 'co-produced'. This meant that the work was to be carried out as a genuine partnership between council social services staff and disabled people, their carers and families.

Each piece of work was also to be co-facilitated with a citizen leader playing a key part in the planning and delivery of the events.

The two pieces of work were:

- outcome focused reviews (OFR) – this work is now complete and the work is published at: http://www.dhcarenetworks.org.uk/Personalisation/ PersonalisationResources/Type/Resource/?cid=5625
- a common resource allocation system (RAS) framework – this work is ongoing.

The two pieces of work were different in scope. The Outcome Focused Reviews work had eight councils represented, with three disabled people and two family carers, while resource allocation had 18 councils and eight disabled people and carers. Tony co-facilitated the OFR project with Helen, and the RAS project with Sam. Co-facilitation with an experienced citizen leader and a consultant working together, and co-production with citizen leaders and councils, were new experiences for each of us. We wanted to record and share what we have learned through this chapter of practical suggestions for others involved in co-production.

We have not gone into the definitions or theory of co-production – these are covered in several papers – instead we share the practical lessons we have learned in preparing for events and facilitating them. We begin with the learning from the OFR work, and then the issues and lessons from the RAS work.

What we learned about co-production in practice

Event set up and design

As we said in the introduction, the Putting People First team commissioned both pieces of work with the explicit intention that they were co-produced and co-facilitated. Many people believe that co-production requires that at least one-third of the group are disabled people, carers or family members. This work was designed to ensure that a third of the participants would be citizen leaders. In the OFR work, it was nearer 50% citizen leaders and 50% council staff. In the RAS work there were fewer citizen leaders – around 25%. The Putting People First team appointed both facilitators separately and convened a meeting for the facilitators to co-design the sessions.

Co-facilitation with a disabled person, carer or family member was a key element to this co-production. It was crucial that both facilitators had the necessary skills and experience to play a full part in the facilitation. We were selected as facilitators for this event through a process of tender or application and interview.

Facilitators

- It is vital that both facilitators share an understanding of the social model of disability and use language that reflects this. The 'medical model' language still in regular use is deeply offensive.
- Both facilitators need to co-design the event and this is even more powerful when participants (a couple of citizen leaders and council staff who will be part of the event) are involved in the design as well, through a 'design team'.
- The facilitators need to have a clear understanding of how they will work together, by discussing how they see their roles, what they bring to this work (their particular skills and interests) and what support they will need from each other. At the reviews events, Tony and Helen talked explicitly about what each expected of the other, and at the RAS events, Sam orchestrated the days and gave specific time-bound tasks to other facilitators.

Participants

- Having the right people, by which we mean people with varied skills and experience that equip them to offer a useful contribution, is absolutely vital. Mere inclusion is just the same as 'consultation' or tokenism. This applies equally to council staff and disabled people. In these pieces of work we invited citizen leaders who had participated in a citizen leadership course and were active in contributing to local and national developments. We invited councils who had expressed an interest in developing reviews or RAS.

Personalisation: Practical thoughts and ideas from people making it happen   © OLM-Pavilion 2009

■ Ensuring a broad spread of disability and experience is important as what is a burning issue to one may be of little or no consequence to another. In these projects there was a dedicated administrator support. A dedicated administrator supported the logistics of the events (including access requirements) and Tony took responsibility for ensuring that the citizen leaders had the information and any support they needed before the work began.

Logistics and budget

■ Equal contribution requires that everyone is paid to attend. Council staff are salaried and you must pay citizen leaders to attend, as well as their expenses, which might include personal assistant costs.

■ It is important to pay attention to logistics, communication and access, and identify someone to take responsibility for this.

Before the events –
what we learned about co-production in practice

Once people had been invited to be part of the work, and the co-facilitators had developed the design, making sure that the initial events were successful required thinking carefully about access and communication.

Access and communication

It is very important to really understand access requirements and ensure that the venue does too.

■ Don't assume – a motorised wheelchair is very different to a self-propelled one and access ramps etc. may not necessarily be adequate. Double check access requirements; are the disabled toilets really accessible? Is the dining room wheelchair friendly? Is an inductive loop installed and working? Is it tested? Equally, don't make assumptions about people; council staff may also have access needs.

■ Working with partially-sighted or blind people means paying attention to differing requirements in the way that material is presented to them in terms of font size, shape and text colour. Again, it is important not to make assumptions and to ask directly what people need. At a recent event that Helen was doing she knew that one person was visually impaired and prepared all the posters for the event with a yellow background, as recommended by the RNIB. She did not realise that for this particular person, yellow was the worst colour background, and when Helen learned this, she managed to get all the posters redesigned with the person's preferred blue background.

- People with access requirements at these events appreciated Tony contacting them to reassure them that we had accommodated their requirements.
- Continue to work with access issues throughout the event by asking people if there is anything else they need and problem-solving any issues. We found out the reception at the venue used for the reviews work was inaccessible for wheelchairs and people using wheelchairs then had to check in separately in the foyer. We talked with the hotel to make them aware of the difficulties this posed and their duties in this area. We discussed this with the citizen leader who uses a wheelchair and considered changing hotels, but ultimately he suggested that we stayed.
- Plan your start and finish times and ensure that you have adequate breaks. In the reviews work we agreed the times and lengths of breaks with participants. Tony negotiated the optimum start and finish time with people before the events, taking into account access and travel times, and the amount of time that we needed to do the work.
- Enable everyone to fully participate by sharing a clear agenda beforehand that helps people to prepare. In the reviews work, we used an agenda format giving the questions we wanted to ask at the event and what we wanted people to think about beforehand. (The agenda format is in the appendix.)

At the events –
what we learned about co-production in practice

- Include everyone right from the beginning by using an opening round. It is typical practice to get people to introduce themselves. In the reviews work we asked people to choose a postcard (from the 50 spread out on the floor) and use it to introduce themselves and say what good co-production meant to them. Beforehand, we talked to the group member with the visual impairment about whether and how we could make this work for her. She asked us to describe a selection of postcards to her and she chose the ones that resonated with her.
- At the reviews events we found it helpful to have a poster of the purpose, agenda, rules and roles (meeting map) up to help everyone to know where they are in the agenda, and how the agenda relates to the purpose of the session. The RAS events had a much larger attendance, but we always outlined the content of the day, and what would be expected of people.
- Agree specific ground rules at the beginning with the group that include paying attention to access issues. In the reviews group we agreed that we would all say our names every time we spoke in the main group, at the request of the group member who has a visual impairment. At the end of the first day we reviewed the ground rules with the group to see how we were doing in practice and whether there were any that people wanted to add.

Personalisation: Practical thoughts and ideas from people making it happen   © OLM-Pavilion 2009

- Adapt facilitation techniques to make them work for everyone. In the reviews work we used a process called a 'card call' where people write on cards and then the whole group clusters them. Rather than not using this approach because someone had a visual impairment, we talked with her about how we could make the process work for her.
- Make sure that everyone is included. At both events we were quite clear that everyone had an equal voice. Occasionally, where relevant, we included PAs in rounds. Some great contributions came from people who were not directly invited to the events – in one case, a supporter became an integral and valuable member of the team.

Getting feedback

In the smaller reviews group we were able to use 'rounds', where everyone was given the opportunity and expected to comment on the current issue. We also used this method for feedback. At the RAS events we asked people to write on two cards about what had been good about the day, and what could have been better. We collated, published and acted on this feedback.

Work between sessions

- Work between events – ensure that everyone has a role to play. At the RAS events where councils were to test material, we involved the disabled people in creating a framework for testing by which they would measure the councils' work. We called it 'What a good testing phase would look like'.

After the events –
what we learned about co-production in practice

The outcome from the OFR event was a report. We worked with the group to think about how everyone wanted to be involved in putting the report together.

- We agreed the potential content areas (based on our earlier work on 'success') for the report and wrote these on a board.
- We asked everyone to think about whether they wanted, or had the time and energy to contribute to writing. This was not an expectation, but an offer to the citizen leaders. Some people wanted to write up stories and another citizen leader wanted to have a first go at the introduction.
- We wanted everyone's contribution and were clear about what was going to happen next, when people would have a chance to review the material, deadlines for comments, and where the overall editorial responsibility was.

Some of this learning was echoed in the RAS work, however, the different nature of the work, the number of people, and the percentage of citizen leaders, led to further learning about building consensus and leadership.

What we learned about co-production in practice an the RAS work

Getting two councils to agree on something can be difficult, so co-producing some complex products related to the creation of personal budgets – with all the passion that goes with it and with 18 councils, some experienced, some not, and also in genuine co-production with disabled people – was a huge, though rewarding challenge. Here are some reflections near to the end of the RAS programme.

Sort out the leadership

■ Culture is powerfully established through leadership. We did not get our co-produced leadership right to begin with. In hindsight this was partly to do with how we were commissioned – separately, with little negotiation or introduction, but also about our own relative lack of experience in relation to co-production. It needed us to make mistakes, reflect, take criticism, and experience some real pressure to deliver in order to create a model of co-produced leadership that really reflected our commitments to joint work. In order to successfully deliver a co-producing environment in the room we had to model and reflect that in the way we led the sessions together.

Model a new relationship

■ Our work was about shifting power and creating new relationships between 'the care system' and disabled people. If we were really committed to this then we had to model it in the way we worked together. For the most part we did our significant work in three working groups, all with representatives of both councils and citizen leaders. Our constant commitment was to minimise the times when we were not 'acting out' our commitment to co-production and joint work. However, we did take one or two opportunities to give time to citizen leaders to agree some key messages that they wanted to give to councils – for instance in the way that councils were, as part of the programme, going to test the materials we were designing together. In this way we established a relationship where disabled people 'directed' public servants – a dynamic we were seeking to support in the materials we were designing.

Positive discrimination

■ The reality of the world, and the social care system as a component of it, is that things are not equal. Disabled people are not listened to properly and individuals don't always get to make the key decisions about their lives. Therefore, it was alright to do a bit of rebalancing every time we met. From the third session onwards – after saying 'hello' to each other – we always started by inviting one or more of the citizen leaders to remind us all why this is important and to ground the work we then did throughout the day in someone's real experience of what counts as respectful social care. This led to some fantastic materials that can be used again – both in written, spoken, and DVD format.

Don't be afraid of the dots

■ We worked hard at establishing good relationships between council employees and disabled people through the way we worked around tables, mixed people up in groups, and had a constant reminder about the agenda we were all committed to. In addition, given the relatively short period of time we had to work in, and the huge challenge to produce useable materials at the end of the programme, sometimes we had to 'cut to the quick'. The group learned together that sometimes in order to reach a consensus we could not continue forever individually articulating a range of views. Also, it was clear that some people were really keen to speak and be heard, and others were less so, but still wanted to contribute.

■ We used a facilitative technique on a number of occasions, which consisted of identifying some key issues (sometimes those that in between sessions were clearly exercising people, given the contributions on the web page), working on them in co-production groups to explore potential solutions, strengths and weaknesses, and then displaying choices on boards so that people could hear about them, read about them, and then indicate through placing their 'dot' where their favoured position lay. We didn't over use it – usually reserving it for issues where we felt we had talked the issue out and needed to move to a conclusion, or where a smaller working group wanted to take direction from the whole group, or where it was absolutely necessary to make a decision in order to move on. We didn't call it 'voting' as this only produces winners and losers. What it did enable us to do was visually display where the feeling of the whole room was – and this shaped the solutions that the working groups then adopted. Of course we had a numbers issue in that there were often about 40 council employees in the room and eight citizen leaders. We adopted a methodology that displayed when a 'dot' was from a council and when a 'dot' was from a citizen leader – by giving them different colour dots. Because we were not voting, and it wasn't first past the post wins, this technique only added to the information that was available, and the scoring process revealed to the whole group the aggregated views of everyone, and aided us in reaching reasonable conclusions that would carry support.

Lots of informal loops to check understanding

■ We made mistakes where we assumed consensus and co-production too early in the journey. Councils are grooved into the concept of 'meetings' with the accompanying and often unwritten rules and expectations. We learnt quickly that it was not alright to work in co-production groups, think we had reached a conclusion, write it up and post it on our web space as work agreed by the group. Several 'loops' of checking things out, by confirming that the decisions the 'author' wrote up were in fact correct representations of where people were at, were necessary.

Time

■ Good co-production takes time! We were constantly being reminded that we were working at a pace that had the potential to threaten real co-production. Working together, ensuring real dialogue and real understanding, and making sure that people have multiple opportunities to check out with each other what they really mean, and that we are happy with the positions we reached, takes time.

Allowing argument

■ We had some lively debates – not just between council employed staff and citizen leaders – but between all possible combinations. Culturally, we are not necessarily skilled at allowing constructive disagreement, which can result either in a 'pretence' of consensus, or outright destructive argument. We had to learn how to allow and encourage disagreement, acknowledge difference, and not force the pace towards consensus.

Constant opportunity to debate, discuss, disagree find consensus – online presence

One of the things we did without really knowing why we were doing it was to establish a private online space where people could continue to debate between meetings, where documents could be posted for comment and where people could ask questions and seek clarification from each other. This turned out to be a vital component of our system to support co-production. It allowed people, at their own pace, to internalise documents, ideas, debates, and contribute. Nobody was excluded from the possibility of inclusion, in contrast to our one-off events where complexity of time, physical environment, audio and visual issues can all conspire against good inclusion.

Build personal relationships

■ Some of what we learnt is just plain good common sense. Quickly building good personal relationships between facilitators and citizen leaders, and also between all participants in the way that sessions were facilitated were very lucrative and wise investments. The evening before each session some of us met in the local pub not to do work, but just to get to know each other a little and it really helped.

Pay attention to language

■ Language is absolutely vital. The 'council environment' has its own language, assumptions and culture. Some of these had to be vigorously challenged, unlearnt, and rethought.

Nail colours to mast – again and again

■ We quickly became aware that there were some key commitments that were non-negotiable and needed to be confirmed and reconfirmed if citizen leaders were going to trust in the process. Hence it was important to visibly and publicly reassert commitment to the social model of disability, to citizenship, to the concept of human rights and self-determination for all people. It was impossible to do this too much.

Conclusion

The two pieces of work taught us a lot about what it means to co-produce work in practice. We have shared the very practical details of setting this up through the OFR work, and how the challenges of building consensus and establishing leadership were managed through the RAS work. We learned that the proportion of disabled people and carers in the room is significant, and that careful attention to how we work together benefits everyone. Our most powerful experiences were the benefits of working together, hearing all views, negotiating differences and ultimately, achieving a much richer and better outcome for everyone.

Appendix – example agenda
Outcome focused reviews

15 January 2009, 10.00am–3.15pm, Jurys Inn Hotel

Time	Agenda item	Who	Outcome	To be prepared before review
10.00	Arrival, sign in and refreshments	Helen and Tony		
10.30	Welcome and introductions. How are we going to work together today?	Tony and Helen	We know who everyone is. We know who is playing what role in the meeting, and agree initial ground rules for the meeting.	Think about ground rules that you would find useful for our work together.
11.00	What is working and not working about reviews at the moment, from your perspective?	Helen	We know what is working and not working from everyone's perspective about reviews at the moment.	Think about your experience of reviews. What is good/works about them? What does not work about them? We will ask you to share this information with everyone by writing your views on a flipchart. Please contact Tony if you may need assistance with this.
11.30	Break			
11.45	What is this programme about? What are we asking you to do?	Martin	Everyone has a clear understanding of what Martin is asking us to do.	

				Think about what an ideal review would be like, from your perspective.
	What is a 'great' review?	Helen	We create our definition of 'success' by describing the principles of great reviews.	
12.20 – 1.15	Lunch			
1.15	What information do reviews need to provide for councils?	Helen	We hear from each council what information or data they need to get from reviews.	Each council to bring a list of their data requirements for reviews, so share with the group. We will write these up on a flipchart.
2.15	Break			
2.30	How have we worked together today, and what do we want to agree for future meetings?	Tony	We review how our meeting has gone today, what has worked about it, and anything that has not worked. We add to our ground rules to address anything that has not worked.	
3.00 – 3.15	What are the next steps? What will we be doing at the residential?	Helen	We have an outline of what we are doing at the residential in February.	

Chapter 14

Citizen leadership: a view from Scotland

The User and Carer Forum, Scotland

*'Users and carers are **citizens**. We expect to be respected as whole people and supported to achieve our aspirations. What needs to happen is that everyone recognises us as their neighbour with the right to be included in society. A good standard of housing and income matters to us and opportunities for employment, the same as everyone else.'*
(Message from the User and Carer Panel to the 21st Century Social Work Review)

The development of citizen leadership

Citizen leadership was developed by the User and Carer Panel, which was brought together as an influencing group for the review of social work services in Scotland. The User and Carer Panel began to meet in 2005 and throughout the year that followed, debated the main issues being considered by the review, such as the role of the social worker and workforce development. It made several presentations to the review group and had a significant influence on the final report, which was published in July 2006 as *Changing Lives* (Scottish Executive, 2006). The review endorsed the Panel's message that *'people who use services can be both inspirational and visionary'*. It declared that the learning from the User and Carer Panel's work should be used *'to develop and embed in practice a new approach to citizen leadership across social work services'* (Scottish Executive, 2006, p68).

The review group accepted the principle that people who use services, and carers, should have support to develop leadership and the *Changing Lives* report indicated that citizen leadership should be exercised at three levels:

- individual, where services should recognise the expertise and strengths of individuals and families
- operational, where *'people who use services and their carers have a significant role to play in the way services are being delivered by being involved in training*

workers, in recruitment and selection and in evaluating and inspecting services'
■   strategic, through involvement in service development and redesign.

Following the review, the new Scottish Government then invited the User and Carer Panel to develop the idea of citizen leadership and how it could be put into practice. Renamed the User and Carer Forum, the group produced the *Principles and Standards of Citizen Leadership*, which was published by the Scottish Government and launched at a national conference in April 2008. The document fleshes out the definition of citizen leadership, establishes its core principles and suggests standards and indicators for putting it into practice. Training in citizen leadership has been piloted in Scottish Borders and North Ayrshire Councils and a DVD and website are in development to support others to adopt this way of working in order to put citizens at the heart of service development.

The members of the original User and Carer Panel and the current Forum collectively have experience of a wide range of social work services, as well as bringing very different life experiences. They describe themselves as follows:

'We are from all over Scotland and have a variety of backgrounds and experiences; these include autism spectrum disorder, caring, criminal justice system, drug and alcohol addiction, dementia, homelessness, learning disability, mental health issues, physical disability, as well as the LGBT (lesbian, gay, bisexual, transgender) and ethnic communities.'

'We are a diverse group of people and we have learned from each other in an atmosphere of mutual respect.' (Scottish Executive, 2006, p69)

As they have worked together, members have developed respect for each other's positions. A strong collective voice has emerged in which individuals each make their own distinctive contribution.

Why must citizen leadership be at the heart of personalisation?

The idea of citizen leadership came out of the Panel's reflections and experiences. Asked to consider what needed to change about services, they felt that the overwhelming need was for staff, professionals and senior managers to listen – listen to individuals and listen to carers. They had many examples of the poor outcomes that resulted when this did not happen. Talking together, they were also aware of the tremendous resources among themselves, resources that could be used for the benefit of people who needed support but who should not have to experience services getting in the way of them living a better life.

They concluded that this change would not come about without a transformation in the relationship between people who required support and people who had the responsibility to organise and provide services. There had to be a shift in power with the agreed aim of ensuring that when services were provided they added value to that individual's life. Many of the critiques and solutions that the Panel brought to the review were ideas that are central to 'personalisation'. In particular, they said that support should enable the person to achieve aspirations, and should be there in time to prevent crises:

'We expect services to make a positive difference to our lives. We are people first. The outcomes we want include having power and control, being able to take risks and contribute to society. This means that there needs to be a shift in power away from people who commission and provide services to service users and carers.'

The Panel and the Forum are clear that they are people first. As citizens they have a right to the support they need to participate individually and collectively and to make a contribution to improving their lives and the lives of others. When considering the qualities of leadership needed for future social work services, they rapidly came to the view that they too could and should be leaders for change. Just as professionals receive opportunities to develop into leadership roles, the User and Carer Forum argues that the leadership potential of people who use services and carers should be developed so that they can exercise greater individual and collective responsibility for the shape of services.

The User and Carer Forum therefore advocate a radical shift in power. They want a new relationship between people who use services and people who deliver support. They expect to be trusted to take risks. They argue that a need for support, for whatever reason, is not an excuse for having your capacity further undermined. Rather, when people are most disempowered, for example, by illness or involuntary receipt of services, every effort should be made to build their capacity for future responsibility. The right support is essential to enable people to take control again. For example, a member with severe and enduring mental health problems told how she found it hard to use the telephone when she was becoming ill. She was able to communicate by email with her social worker in that situation so that she could be admitted rapidly for treatment and this way was able to avoid extended periods of crisis.

Citizen leadership is about 'leading together'. It is a model of collaborative working between people who use services, informal carers and paid workers. Citizen leaders want empowered staff and one of their criticisms of social work services is how disempowered social workers have become. The definition of leadership put forward by the User and Carer Forum is an enabling one. *'A leader influences and enables others to make a contribution and so helps to make it happen.'* (User and Carer Forum, 2008, p4:5)

Nor is citizen leadership about every man or woman for themselves. The idea came from very different people working and talking together in a group. They recognise collective advocacy as a powerful example of citizen leadership in action. There are many examples from the Forum itself of people actively engaging with the concern of others. The oldest member of the Forum is very interested in the issues faced by young carers. The Panel and Forum themselves demonstrate the enormous reserves of energy and commitment that very busy people, with many issues in their own lives, can bring to try and make things better for others. As Isabel, a Forum member notes:

'The reason why I want to be on this Forum is in the hope we can help with ideas and actions so that users, carers and providers do not have to wait in vain for the spirit of the agenda set out in Changing Lives to influence the delivery of improved services.'

The spirit and practice of citizen leadership are key to making personalisation a reality. The Scottish Government has defined personalisation as:

'It enables the individual alone, or in groups, to find the right solutions for them and to participate in the delivery of a service. From being a recipient of services, citizens can become actively involved in selecting and shaping the services they receive.' (Changing Lives Service Development Group, 2009, p10).

The Scottish Government acknowledges (p12) that personalisation needs to be owned by users and carers. Their paper on personalisation stresses the need for dialogue and for people and professionals working together to manage risks and resources. Citizen leadership then states what users and carers want and need to develop the capacity to engage with the agenda. Fundamental to that engagement is the determination that it should lead to person-centred solutions.

What does citizen leadership look like?

There are eight principles of citizen leadership (see **box 1**). The principles and standards paint a picture of how things might be different if people were really at the heart of services, influencing decisions about their own support and also contributing to service design for others.

In the first place, nobody would be written off. The person in acute crisis or the person who has committed an offence would not be stripped of all autonomy. It would be a priority to re-engage them and to find ways to restore their responsibility when they were able. It would be a responsibility not only to protect but also to maximise the capacity of the person with dementia, however small and individual the ways in which they could be supported to be in control.

Box 1: The principles of citizen leadership		
1.	**Potential**	Everyone should have their leadership potential recognised.
2.	**Development**	People's leadership potential can only be fulfilled through opportunities for development.
3.	**Early involvement**	People who use services and carers must be involved at all stages of developing and delivering services.
4.	**Person-centred**	Everyone is an individual and should be helped to show leadership in the way that suits them best.
5.	**Information**	People need information that is clear to them and they need it in plenty of time.
6.	**Equality**	People use their leadership skills to challenge inequality in services and the wider society.
7.	**Control through partnership**	Citizen leadership enables people to have more control over their own services, through working in partnership with those services.
8.	**Wider benefit**	Citizen leadership is for the benefit of other people who use services as well as yourself.

Because people were seen as partners there would be investment in ensuring that they could participate as fully as possible, and disinvestment in processes that kept people distant from decision-making. People who had used services would be acting as mentors to others and there would be many role models of successful citizen leaders. Professionals would find themselves alongside people who use services and carers in person-centred planning training and in briefing sessions for service redesign. Indeed, they would be trained by them. All professionals would learn skills in enabling people with a wide range of preferred communication methods to participate. They would see their role as allowing others to share their expertise, not just as expressing their own view.

One of the most visible changes would be in the way the day-to-day business of developing services was carried out. The indicators for the principle of early involvement show the kind of changes that the User and Carer Forum expect. If people who use services and carers are to be involved at all stages in the development and delivery of services, the meetings where people are asked for their views will take place at accessible community venues and other places that are easy to get to. When it

becomes clear that people's views are wanted and are acted upon, then people will become more confident in challenging professionals but also the number of positive suggestions about change will increase.

Citizen leadership is about more than participation. Nonetheless, the experience of the User and Carer Panel suggested some important ingredients for successful engagement. **Box 2** shows what the Panel considered to be essential for successful participation.

Box 2: The ingredients of successful participation
■ independent facilitation
■ ground rules
■ respect
■ attention to the needs of participants, especially communication needs
■ information that is summarised and presented in an accessible way
■ good venues
■ expenses paid on the day
■ commitment from the top to take our views on board.

The User and Panel was itself an example of citizen leadership because:

■ people who used services influenced services at a policy level
■ they were involved in the process at an early stage
■ they negotiated a certain amount of power
■ they had leadership skills to communicate what they wanted to say
■ they had the chance to develop new skills and confidence along the way – attributes they can use in other situations.

Finally, commissioners would find themselves working alongside citizens to help influence the changes needed for a more equal and inclusive society. Together they would challenge the language and processes of other agencies (and their own) that left some people out. They would ask why public resources were not being spent to ensure that everyone had access and they would demonstrate together how advocacy

for disabled and excluded people can bring investment into communities and model ways of doing things differently to the benefit of all community members. An example is the work of the local area co-ordination service in the east of Glasgow. Here the people with learning disabilities and parents who lead the work were able to see the priorities they had expressed influencing the work of local agencies. The local area co-ordinator helped a voluntary organisation to obtain £22,000 in additional funding and take forward three new initiatives. The community gained and the organisation's work was targeted on local needs (Scottish Government, 2008).

The standards of citizen leadership also give some indications of what is needed to make citizen leadership work. If people are to have greater control and influence they must receive support that enables them to tackle the problems and issues that are preventing them from taking more control over their own lives. Paid services must not get in the way of people having lives and relationships. Deficit-based assessments need to give way to self-assessments and assessments that identify people's strengths and gifts. Citizens need to be equipped with information and to have the means to share information themselves through peer networks and other means. This presupposes a much more open culture in which information about mistakes as well as good practice can be shared. It is essential that all citizens have the appropriate support to communicate and participate and that clear standards are enforced to make information accessible. These are some of the foundations on which capacity can be built. Citizen leadership also presupposes some key rights – to choose the provider of services, to select workers and to have access to opportunities to develop skills.

Conclusion

In conclusion, personalisation is not something that can be done to people. It is essential that legislators, pundits and professionals really see people who require support as partners in finding solutions to the issues they face in their lives. This is a matter of justice. However, efficiency as well as effectiveness also requires that the people who know best about their own lives should have a considerable influence over the best way.

'If we as citizens have more say over the services we receive, there is more chance that these services will be right for us. When this happens they will be more likely to produce the outcomes we are looking for' (User and Carer Forum, 2008, 14:15).

The User and Carer Forum has not ignored the challenges that this proposal presents. They are aware of the pressures on health and social care organisations to protect the public and to prevent wherever possible the abuse and exploitation of vulnerable people. However, their point is that you are most likely to enable people to live safe and fulfilling lives when you support them to overcome the obstacles

and maximise their capacity for responsibility. Citizen leadership sees responsibility for good outcomes as a shared responsibility; for this to happen requires trust. The capacity for bold change must be developed among people who use services, carers, professionals and the public.

References

Changing Lives Service Development Group (2009) *Personalisation: A shared understanding.* Edinburgh: The Scottish Government.

Scottish Executive (2006) *Changing Lives: Report of the 21st century social work review* [online]. Edinburgh: Blackwell. Available at: http://www.scotland.gov.uk/Publications/2006/02/02094408/0 (accessed August 2009).

Scottish Government (2008) *National Guidance on the Implementation of Local Area Co-ordination* [online]. Available at: http://www.scotland.gov.uk/Publications/2008/03/27092411/0 (accessed August 2009).

User and Carer Forum, Scottish Government (2008) *Principles and Standards of Citizen Leadership.* Edinburgh: Blackwell.

Chapter 15

Personalisation and the law

Belinda Schwehr

There is no doubt that personalisation offers local authorities and their social care service users a new way of working – but no new major piece of legislation is being introduced to underpin the manner in which the new policy will be presented across 150 local authorities. This chapter considers the implications of this very English way of doing things in 2009.

Local authorities do what they do within their social services departments because of **law** – and this author's view is that it can't hurt to know some, when you are faced with acronyms like the RAS (resource allocation system), SDS (self-directed support) and UIT (user independent trust), or new concepts, such as 'individual service funds' and 'virtual managed accounts', and new processes such as the 'risk enablement panel' … and 'Shop4Support'.

Since they are spending your money and mine, local authorities can only do things that are made lawful by Acts of Parliament, regulations, directions and guidance from the Department of Health, and which accord with the developing case law judgments coming out of judges' mouths in disputed court cases. They can't just do things because it seems like a good idea at the time.

Knowing about all that stuff, understanding it and making sure that one's department is complying with the implications of it, is what obeying the law actually **means** for a director of adult services. But most local authority directors trained and became professionals in an era when there was hardly any litigation changing the legal pathways to delivering social care, and they may well have been too busy to go to legal framework training courses since then. Most local authority lawyers would have been trained in child care law only and not adult services law. So without intending to denigrate any particular local authority's commitment to doing it lawfully, this author would still consider it legitimate to say that it's not unusual to find that what the law **requires**, on the one hand, and the reality of the content of departmental practice and

pilots, in a culture of performance management within local authorities, have often long since parted company.

In this author's view, 'choice' and 'citizenship', without knowledge, don't equate to anything that feels like actual power or security. The extent of a **right** to social care is a measure of something valuable in any society, and there are no rights without law and legal remedies.

Raising the profile of the importance of the pros and cons of personalisation is the only way to kindle debate, in my view – debate about something on which, at some point in the future, each one of us may have no option but to depend upon. The law **can** make us all more equal, but it will only work to do so in this particular field if social care is administered with regard to it, and not in spite of it.

And since vulnerable adults tend not to bite the hand that funds them, for fear of being left with needs they are unable to meet for themselves, or, at the very least, souring a long-term relationship of dependency on the local authority, there would **always** have been a strong possibility of arbitrariness in the wake of Putting People First.

On top of all that, those in charge of hypothesising about the best way forward have regarded the current system as broken, unworkable, and paternalistic, and have vociferously suggested that transformation cannot occur without wholesale and radical reform.

Babies and bathwater come to mind, in the sense that there is much **good** in the current system, which an informed disabled person would not want to throw out, at least not without thinking about the implications for themselves and others, first of all.

Here are some basic principles of the law relating to local authorities and to social services in particular, which have been developed by the legal system over the last half century. First of all:

■ A local authority cannot use departmental lack of money as an excuse for not **assessing** needs for social care, not **providing** appropriately for assessed eligible needs, or for making someone wait, if the person has been assessed as having eligible needs, purely because of shortage of money within the departmental coffers. This is because all these things are duties, as opposed to discretions (ie. things that a local authority **must** do, as opposed to having a discretionary choice, informed by local politics and priorities).

Personalisation: Practical thoughts and ideas from people making it happen   © OLM-Pavilion 2009

And second, a local authority **must** act in the following ways.

- **Not irrationally,** in the discharge of its functions. So it is not possible for a social worker to say 'One toileting visit a week will be enough' – judges have got bladders of their own, as a benchmark of the good sense or otherwise, of that sort of an opinion.
- **In accordance with human rights**, properly understood. It is not possible for a local authority to assume that everyone's relative is benign, well-informed, non-abusive and non-conflicted with the person for whom the authority would otherwise have to make arrangements. Nor to ignore **dignity** as a concept of relevance (albeit a woolly one) in the determination of how much care a person needs, or from how many carers.
- **Without fettering its own discretion, and procedurally fairly** – ie. giving people a fair crack at persuading a local authority in matters of subtlety or opinion, and not sticking rigidly to particular positions. So it is not fair to say that a resource allocation is an 'indicative guideline' only but not tell anyone how to challenge the sum to which the number crunching has given rise. Nor is it fair to say that people must use the complaint system as a means of challenging 'first' when the essence of the complaint here would be that the authority hasn't even done its own legal duty properly, which is to decide **rationally** how much money is needed to meet the eligible assessed need.
- **Within the confines of what is permitted for it to do by statutes or regulations** so a local authority cannot make an incapacitated person's mother into their lawfully authorised **agent**, attorney or deputy, just by calling them a 'representative', for the purposes of managing the person's direct payment (even though the incapacitated person will be able to have a direct payment, at the behest of a relative or friend, notwithstanding their inability to consent to one, personally, once the new law comes into effect in late 2009). Another example is that the local authority can't ignore the fact that undertakings given money under certain statutory functions operate as agents of the council, whatever the contract says, and are obliged to register as a domiciliary care agency if they arrange personal care for people who cannot do it for themselves (unless excepted by the regulations).
- **And otherwise lawfully** – ie. not ignoring manual handling regulations, or the Choice of Accommodation Directions and Guidance, or the Assessment Directions 2004, or the Equalities and Diversity obligations in local government law, or health and safety rules, or the Mental Capacity Act and its application to the need for capacity before a tenancy can be organised for someone (unless they have a deputy or attorney), or the rules on deprivation of liberty, for instance.

In relation to personalisation, here are some pointers to follow that can help to build a lawful and sustainable personalised system.

■ Care management needs to be accountable to professionally qualified supervision, even if more responsibility for the earlier part of the process is delegated to people who have merely been trained and/or inducted into the values of social work and the social model of disability and person-centred care planning. Co-production of a support plan, as between the authority and the recipient of the money or services, should be the ultimate aim of the system.

■ Care planning for those who do not want to make suggestions as to how it should be done, can be contributed to by the private sector provider, whose contract binds the provider to do what the care plan says, in the first place; but it cannot be delegated to the provider altogether. Local authority sign-off of support plans, risk management plans and other details is a good way of being accountable in a transparent way.

■ Contract monitoring of council contracts is still an essential function. The duty to meet need is not delegable. Contracts staff, in a new personalised world, may come to be a valuable resource for liaising cost-effectively, and lawfully, between the market and the service users – either as local authority officers for those wanting a virtual managed account, or as private persons' **agents**, for those wanting that sort of help to manage their direct payment.

■ Resource allocation systems (the approach to dividing up the funding) should allow for further refinement and change to the eventual personal budget, once a support plan has been designed for an individual. This is good common sense as well as necessary in legal terms. There is no prospect of a scientifically exact calculation capable of being done in advance of considering the individual's situation because, most obviously, it will not be known in advance whether that person has family and carers who are willing and able to help support that person.

■ Consultation about and publicising of the authority's thinking behind its approach to resource allocation should be the rule, and freedom of information principles provide a framework for this, because this thought process constitutes the **policy** of elected representatives in each authority's area.

■ It shouldn't be the case that people are told that they can only have a resource allocation fixed by reference to the resource allocation system and the answers on their assessment form (ie. that it is a take-it-or-leave-it amount, or a full discharge of social care duties). The new system should represent a 'first response' to potential need, and one which does not shut off access to one's legal rights. Good practice is emerging around RASs delivering 'indicative amounts', which then get tested through supported planning and risk enablement panels for the few for whom it does not represent a better or a lawful social care outcome.

Personalisation: Practical thoughts and ideas from people making it happen   © OLM-Pavilion 2009

- Potential applicants for social care support must be able to see the relationship between the local eligibility threshold for provision under Fair Access to Care Services, the questions about various domains of a person's life in a needs-based questionnaire, and the scope of social care legal duties, that all contribute to a preliminary view about eligibility for an individual budget. People deserve a fair chance to persuade an authority that they meet criteria, and this requires information about the benchmarks and approach to evaluating a person's answers.

- It is human nature to change one's mind after actually experiencing something. Local authorities and potential clients must both accept this. Those in receipt of an offer of a budget need to be willing to 'try it and see', where it is reasonable to expect this, because an authority needs to be able to make an informed decision as to whether or not the budget and the support plan leave the person with unlawful unmet need for social care services. The only rational way to do this is to try it and see, and set practical review dates for considering the outcome.

- Processes for challenging the indicative amount should be embedded into the system, rather than dissent at an interim stage being seen as a complaint or an allegation of legal wrongdoing. Strong management will be competent and brave enough to make principled exceptions, the grounds for which will be broadly publicised in advance.

- What constitutes an assessment is not prescribed by statute or case law, and is allowed in government guidance to be a proportionate process in light of the person's presenting situation. However, it does include someone who is employed or lawfully authorised by the local authority coming to a conclusion about presence of needs that constitute above-threshold risks to independence. Section 47 also requires a conclusion about potential needs for other agencies' services so that the person can be referred correctly for a decision by those agencies. An assessment incorporates both the decision about eligibility and the identification of what the authority thinks is appropriate to do, provide or arrange for, so as to meet those acknowledged needs. In an SDS approach this requirement may be able to be met by the sign-off of the RAS in light of the support plan agreed, by someone employed or authorised by the local authority.

- There is growing awareness that resource allocations for social care purposes cannot be cut for individuals, halfway through the financial year, when the going gets tough, because the meeting of need for eligible individuals is a duty. The legal position is different for an authority's discretionary functions, such as the funding of well-being services under s2 Local Government Act (2000), and this gives some room for budget management to local authorities during a financial year. Any changes to existing allocations will require a new sign-off by the authority as outlined above.

- Resource allocation **formulae** shouldn't differ for people coming into the system at different times during the financial year – unless consultation processes and consideration of equalities and diversities duties in relation to raising the applicable Fair Access to Care Services threshold have been followed.
- Individuals' resource allocations should be altered at reasonable intervals by reference to relevant inflation indices, as a matter of course. Reviews of assessments should be done at least annually, as is required by government guidance, and a review of assessment offers the chance to adjust the amount on an evidenced basis.
- In relation to social care needs, it is needs for services that have to be delivered upon, by the individual and/or their chosen provider, not outcomes or needs in general. Broader use of an individual budget for well-being purposes, however, need not be so rigorously constrained.
- There should be clarity over what it is acceptable to the local authority to spend the money on and what it must NOT be spent on, including **who** it can be spent on, as well as on what.
- There should be clear agreements between private providers and members of the public (eg. on online local authority organised websites for local support sources) and between service users with less than full capacity, and their brokers or 'helpers' or providers.
- There should be clarity about the status of monies left over at the end of any budget period in an individual's personal budget, as it will either represent **over**-assessed needs, in which case it must be handed back or rolled over to the next period, or alternatively it will constitute under-**spent** monies, in relation to accurately **assessed** needs, over which there **may** be a legitimate reason for the individual to retain control, for contingencies.
- There should be clarity about the residual responsibility of authorities if the money that has been handed over has been dissipated before it is time for a fresh injection – in cases of sheer bad luck, imprudence, exploitation, abuse or out-and-out badly intentioned collusion with a wrongdoer, for instance, the reason for the problem will have a bearing on the responsibilities of those concerned. These 'what-ifs' could be built into good support planning.
- Safeguarding responsibilities remain the same and need to be taken seriously. Commitment to personalisation also requires clarity and hard-headed thinking about how these responsibilities are capable of discharge in the context of a much more arm's length relationship, despite some of the beneficiaries of the policy lacking in mental capacity.

Personalisation: Practical thoughts and ideas from people making it happen   © OLM-Pavilion 2009

If people or family members think that personalisation is being used to operate illegally or improperly, and you cannot get anybody in the local authority to listen, respond, or satisfy your concern, there are things you can do without having to seek legal advice or spend money or find an advocate.

■ Write a short letter to the authority's monitoring officer, usually the head lawyer, pointing out as comprehensively as you can what you think the authority is doing in breach of the law and explaining its impact on you or your family member. Give names, ages, client group, social work key workers' names, and details of any existing care packages, and ask for his or her response as a matter of urgency, on whether it is agreed that what's going on could be a breach of the law. Ask that if it is the provisional view, the monitoring officer assures you that he or she will stop it happening, pending a proper investigation.

You will find that writing to the monitoring officer engages the brain and focus of senior staff, and that you will save much time and effort in using this route in circumstances where there really is something legally less than ideal going on.

If this doesn't work, write to the local and national newspapers. Government policy about social services **is** a matter of politics, but the trade-off between peoples' legal rights, the way the current system works (or does not work) and the prospect of more room to exercise autonomy and personal choice under the new vision has not received much coverage in the country's serious newspapers as yet.

Personalisation is a matter of politics as well – because to some people, it will seem to be a proposal to give those dependent on public money more of what they **want**, as well as what they need.

Even if that's not a fair summation (because it should be seen instead to be about making sure the support that people **need** is delivered in a way that actually works for people) then clearly relevant to the rationale behind a workable RAS is whether people's carers will cope between the high points of a dependent person's day when they are accessing presumed-to-be adequate mainstream services, or spending their budget on higher quality or more expensive paid services, as the pilots have shown that people tend to want to do.

Carers are women, in the main, and women now work, in the main, from educational aspiration, choice, or economic necessity. So incentivising them to **want** to become, or not **mind** becoming care managers, care providers or care brokers should be a major plank in any political party's manifesto, I would have thought. Limiting the vision, by the

requirement for it to be cost-neutral from the outset, may not send a credible enough message about the feasibility of real change and its likely benefits to these people.

It may be the position that no government can come up with any better way of coping with the changing demographics and numbers of those who **need** social care subsidised and arranged by the state. But if that isn't a political matter, worthy of debate, then I don't know **what** a political party would have to do to make us all sit up and take notice.

Chapter 16

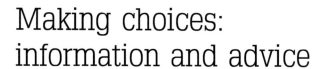

Making choices:
information and advice

Steven Rose

This chapter is dedicated to the memory of John and Muriel Rose

Only four years ago when my parents needed support over and above the sheltered accommodation and domiciliary support they had been receiving, their care manager gave me an internet print out of several hundred nursing and residential homes and left my brother and I to get on with things. At the time, I had worked in the health and social care sector for over 30 years. For the previous 15 years I had been the chief executive of a national learning disability charity, prior to that I had been a director of nursing in the NHS and more recently spent five years as a non-executive director of my local primary care trust. My knowledge and experience of the health and social care system was vast. Yet, when I suddenly became a representative of service users I was faced with a daunting task, little information and what felt like an impersonal and uncaring system. My brother and I struggled to get a decent service for my parents. All we wanted was for them to be together at an affordable location convenient for us and other family members to pay frequent visits. Eventually, we found a service that suited both of my parents' needs and allowed them, after over 60 years of happily married life to spend their remaining 18 months in this world, together.

In spite of my vast experience of the health and social care system, I struggled to get a decent service for my parents. Eventually, the local authority adopted a more reasonable attitude after my parents' local MP intervened on their behalf. Aside from being left exhausted, frustrated and angry, I was left with a strong feeling of disbelief at how many unnecessary obstacles had been put in our way. I was also deeply concerned. If my brother and I, who are both reasonably educated, articulate and when necessary, assertive people, who had the added advantage of my knowledge of the system, had struggled so hard, what was the experience of others – people who may not be so well-positioned as we were to challenge the inadequacies of the social care system?

'Personalisation', giving the opportunity to service users and/or their representatives to direct their own support, is already offering empowering alternatives to the situation I found myself in. The power of consumerism is set to prevail. In 2006 there were just 60 people with a personal budget. By March 2009 there were 12,000 people with a personal budget, plus a further 70,000 receiving a direct payment (Duffy, 2009).

However, having control of one's own budget is of limited use if there is not a good range of products to choose from. At the moment, many of the social care products available are the traditional products (eg. residential care) and there is little point in controlling your own budget if all you can buy is what you would have got under the old system. The social care market is gradually changing with more and more new and innovative solutions becoming available.

This chapter aims to point the reader contemplating directing their own services through an individual budget, whether they be a service user or representative of a service user, to places where they can get assistance and advice. It also addresses some of the practical issues around making choices and managing your own support. Managing your own support can be a daunting prospect and many people are unsure of where to turn to for information, advice and support. All of the organisations listed in this chapter are likely to be able to help in one way or another. Those seeking help in making choices could consider support brokerage.

For those contemplating employing their own (PAs) personal assistant/s, a new organisation is now providing the first national voice for disabled people who employ personal assistants. Staying on the right side of employment legislation is difficult enough for large employers who employ human resource professionals and often turn to specialist lawyers for advice. For the disabled person without previous experience of employment legislation, staying on the right side of the law can be something akin to navigating your way through a minefield. The organisation ADE provides advice and information, and a forum for members to share ideas, as well as campaigning for disabled people to have more control over issues around PAs, personalisation and independent living. It provides support for any disabled person who employs a PA, support worker or carer, whether through direct payments, access to work or private funding. ADE aims to be a strong voice for disabled people who employ their own staff, and to achieve a national voice for disabled people who employ their own staff so they will not feel isolated and they will feel they are being listened to. Details of the ADE organisation can be found at www.beingtheboss.co.uk.

In Control

In Control is a social enterprise that was set up to transform the current social care system into a system of self-directed support. Its stated mission is to create a new welfare system in which everyone is in control of their lives as full citizens.

Personalisation: Practical thoughts and ideas from people making it happen   © OLM-Pavilion 2009

In Control is a partnership working with different kinds of friends and allies, for example, citizen members, local authority and NHS members, providers, commercial organisations, sponsors and ambassadors. Its members include 120 adult social care departments, 24 children departments and 37 NHS primary care trusts. In Control's intellectual property is developed by its membership and is free for its members to use. This methodology for supporting innovation is efficient, sustainable and empowering. In Control's website: www.in-control.org.uk remains the leading source of expertise and information on self-directed support.

The Big Event

The Big Event is run each year by In Control and is the biggest live showcase for self-directed support in the UK. It's aimed at everyone and anyone who wants self-directed support to happen in their community. In March 2009, over 1,000 people with an interest in self-directed support attended the Big Event, which was held at the Business Design Centre in Islington, London.

The Big Event includes:

- keynote addresses by experts in the field
- a live market place consisting of a wide range of exhibitors large and small to enable delegates to network, pick up new ideas, think differently and shop for the help
- a live help desk and advice line consisting of the best people in the UK who know how to make self-directed support happen
- and many, many interactive workshops on how to make self-directed support work for everyone including interactive support planning, developing the market, building community capacity, interactive drama sessions, social innovation and enterprise, managing risk, speakers' corner and what we have learned so far, to name a few.

Details of the 2010 Big Event can be found on the In Control website (www.in-control. org.uk/bigevent/).

Service brokerage

There is currently considerable debate about what service brokerage is. Most of this debate focuses on whether service brokerage is a separate, independent and discreet function carried out by independently funded 'professional' service brokers or whether brokerage is largely a function that can be carried out by a wider group (eg. family, friends, provider organisations, care managers etc).

The concept of service brokerage is not a new one. However, the debate around it has been revitalised by the self-directed support agenda. The late David Brandon

wrote extensively about service brokerage in *Community Living* magazine in the 1980s (see Brandon, 1989). He was writing about models of service brokerage emerging in Canada at the time. One of the original Canadian projects was the Vancouver Service Brokerage Project. The model was simple. Service users had an individual financial allocation. The Service Brokerage Project was a state funded agency that provided independent service brokers to assist the disabled person to navigate their way around the system and negotiate the service/s they wanted. A number of service brokerage projects in the UK were modelled on the Vancouver Project. Much was written about the Vancouver Project and the UK projects in the late 1980s and early 1990s (Rose, 1994), however, none of them survived.

The Vancouver Project

Today, as stated above, there is considerable debate about what service brokerage is. Traditionalists cling to the view that the service broker must be entirely independent and independently funded.

One such body is the National Brokerage Network that states, *'The National Brokerage Network (NBN) is a "network of networks" that has been set up to act as an information exchange and an authoritative voice for the development of brokerage throughout the UK.*

'It aims to represent the views and interests of the diverse support broker movement with key politicians and policy makers. It hopes to build and grow an authoritative body to provide strong leadership, drive and guidance in development of brokerage. The NBN hopes to be able to offer and co-ordinate training by using the specialist skills of broker members.' For more information see the National Brokerage Network website (http://www.nationalbrokeragenetwork.org.uk/index.html).

However, increasingly provider organisations are offering brokerage services. One of the first to do so was Choice Support (www.choicesupport.org.uk), which offers a free brokerage service. Other provider organisations are beginning to follow this trend.

A pragmatic view would be that while it may be desirable to have legions of entirely independent and skilled service brokers, for two reasons, this simply is not going to happen. First, there will be no new money to fund brokerage and few people in receipt of individual budgets or direct payments will not be able to afford brokers' fees. Second, there is not anything like the number of skilled people available to create this new workforce or 'profession'. The reality is that most brokerage is already being carried out by family, friends, provider organisations, care managers etc. and this trend is likely to continue.

This is also the view put forward in the report on In Control's second phase and an extract from the report is reproduced here (Hatton *et al*, 2008, pp62–63).

Personalisation: Practical thoughts and ideas from people making it happen   © OLM-Pavilion 2009

Support brokerage

There has been a great deal of discussion about 'support brokerage' as a preferred method to enable people to plan and organise social care and to live a full life. There is a growing body of knowledge about brokerage in the UK, largely situated in those local authorities that are members of In Control, and there are lessons to be drawn from international experience. Yet definitions and understanding of what defines support brokerage remain contested or unclear. Indeed, the use of the term has become so broad as to be described as an *'international shorthand for the kind of interpreters of a system which recipients may welcome'*. Further important questions exist about who should provide brokerage, how it can best be developed, delivered and funded.

It may be more helpful to think about 'support brokerage' as a set of tasks or functions, rather than a role. These include:

- assisting the person to develop a vision of how he or she wants to live
- reviewing, preparing and/or identifying indicative costs of creating and implementing a support plan
- clarifying the person's needs and expectations, including, in the light of the local authority's assessment, eligibility criteria under *Fair Access to Care*
- identifying and applying for funding from all government and non-government sources
- supporting the *Fair Access to Care* appeals process if required
- identifying and enabling the person to access community resources
- assisting with funding negotiation with commissioners
- liaising and negotiating with support providers, monitoring and evaluating support and modifying existing supports or developing new ones
- mediating and resolving problems (as directed by the person).

A support broker can be understood as a specialist in carrying out these functions, an independent professional who can help with planning and who is not involved in providing support or rationing resources. However, other people and organisations may also be well placed to carry out some or all of these functions.

As noted, some people have undertaken these activities entirely for themselves, or (more frequently) with family support. Care managers have continued to play a very considerable role in supporting people to plan and organise their support. Some people have received this assistance from a specialist support broker, typically employed by a voluntary sector agency or working freelance. In other instances independent advocates, service providers, centres for independent living or direct payment schemes have undertaken these functions.

Developmental strategies for brokerage must take account of the range of different parties that can provide this support. It is clear that strategies to develop support brokerage must engage at a number of different levels in order to ensure that people have a choice of different support brokerage options.

It is also clear that deliberate strategies need to be formulated and implemented to develop brokerage. A laissez-faire approach risks assistance not being available to people to plan and arrange support. Alternatively, such an approach may result in dominance over support brokerage by care managers or large providers. These groups have the resources to invest in developing brokerage and have some obvious incentives to do so. Both outcomes would be unhelpful and may limit the potential of self-directed support.

A five-point strategy for the development of support brokerage is therefore suggested. As described below, action is required to:

1. enable people and families to take their own decisions
2. enable user-led organisations and community groups to play a full role
3. shape support providers' contribution.
4. focus care management
5. promote the development of independent support brokerage.

Shop4Support

The internet, as we all know, is fast becoming the preferred way to shop – so why should shopping for support, equipment, services or local community information be any different?

Shop4Support® is a social enterprise based online marketplace that is majority owned by In Control and that has been developed by Valueworks, based upon their industry leading eCommerce platform. The core purpose of Shop4Support is to enable the creation of a retail marketplace for health and social support that creates better value for citizens through offering a choice of focused services and by helping them to control their support, their money and their lives.

The attraction of Shop4Support for the key stakeholder groups is that it provides a software system that meets the requirements of each individual stakeholder group while at the same time providing a common platform that rapidly results in the effective transformation of adult social care at a local level. The benefits of Shop4Support are the ability of:

- **individuals** and their brokers to manage/administer their support plans, personal budgets and relationships with service providers
- **service providers** to easily market their services and manage the new back-office processes required to operate in a retail environment
- **local authorities** to improve commissioning and strengthen the local market, and to manage the new personalisation business processes, in order to ensure that a transformation occurs efficiently and effectively.

The operating model underpinning Shop4Support is encapsulated in **figure 1**.

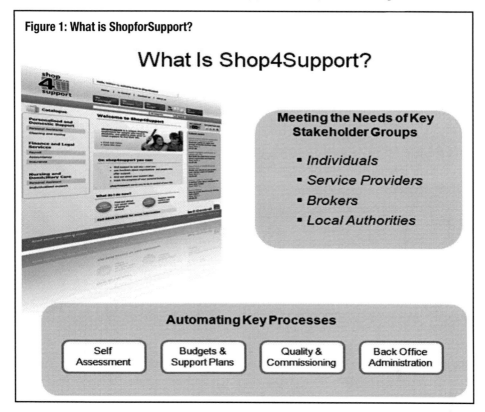

Figure 1: What is ShopforSupport?

What Is Shop4Support?

Meeting the Needs of Key Stakeholder Groups

- *Individuals*
- *Service Providers*
- *Brokers*
- *Local Authorities*

Automating Key Processes

| Self Assessment | Budgets & Support Plans | Quality & Commissioning | Back Office Administration |

More details of Shop4Support are available at **www.shop4support.com** and the first phase implementation report on Shop4Support at **www.in-control.org.uk**.

Self Direct

Self Direct is a social enterprise and consists of a small central team and a wider network of associates. Self Direct associates are people with real life experience of how social and health care services affect lives. They aim to support people with real life experience to drive forward the changes in the social and health marketplace.

Self Direct's work focuses on two main areas.

- When people get their individual budgets, what is there for them to 'buy'?
- What does self-directed support and individual budgets mean for providers, how do providers have to change the way they work?

Self Direct works with a wide range of individuals with a disability or needing health or social care. They state:

'Whether someone needing this support and information is a person with a learning disability, a physical disability, someone who needs support with mental health problems, with sensory impairments or an older person with health or social support needs, we believe the changes that Self Direct promotes should help people to get a life that's right for them. Self Direct is also here for their allies and people who support them, their friends, families, carers and professionals.'

Self Direct also focuses on helping provider organisations respond to the personalisation agenda and runs provider events to help promote change.

Self Direct is a partner of In Control. On the Self Direct website (www.selfdirect.org) you can also comment on blogs posted by Self Direct associates and team members.

Community Connecting magazine

Community Connecting magazine is published six times a year and is the only publication in the UK dedicated to promoting the personalisation agenda. The magazine was launched in 2005 as a learning disability publication. In 2008 the editorial decision was made to restrict most of the magazine to articles promoting the personalisation agenda and to gradually widen coverage to the whole of social care. For enquiries and subscriptions contact: kate@hawkerpublications.com.

Paradigm

Paradigm is a consultancy, training and development agency. Paradigm works with local authorities, support providers, education and health services, disabled people and their families. All of their work is based on the aim of ensuring that people can lead the lives they want. They provide training, publish books, give advice, provide coaching and practical help for services to change, host a website with a wealth of resources and run conferences. Every conference has free places for people with learning difficulties. Paradigm played a very significant role in getting self-directed support and individual budgets introduced in the UK and helped to set up In Control, providing many of their initial staff. They have been at the forefront of many exciting developments in the UK, including supported living, person-centred planning and people and families being in control. Paradigm is driven by a very clear set of values, is passionate about what they do and always work to make a real positive difference in the lives people lead. For more information about Paradigm see their website (www. paradigm-uk.org), email admin@paradigm-uk.org, or call 0870 0104933.

Housing Options

As well as needing direct support, people need a place to live and if you need expert support in finding somewhere to live try Housing Options. Housing Options Advisory Service was set up 10 years ago to provide advice and information for people with learning difficulties, their families and others.

It grew out of a project looking at home ownership. What it found were examples of new ideas for finding your own home, created by families, or support providers and housing associations responding to the needs of people they were working with. The project produced a report with case study examples and guidance on ownership options.

What was also evident from the work was that it was important to share ideas and information. Where could families or concerned professionals go for help with finding a place to live? Housing Options was set up to provide an answer.

Housing Options Advisory Service has a core of member organisations who both support and benefit from the work of the service. It was set up to promote ideas for living that go beyond residential care options to other forms of supported housing, renting, low cost home ownership and use of family investment or property. It is a charity aiming to provide independent advice to disabled people, carers and professionals.

Moving to settled accommodation

For accommodation and services there has been a major shift from institutional to 'community care' services. First people were moved from long-stay hospitals to community homes, often registered care homes. But the Community Care Act guidance 10 years ago said the aim was for people to have care in their own homes. Increasingly, registered care, though still the predominant service option, was joined by 'supported housing' services. You had your own home, usually through a housing association, charity or council tenancy and you had support and care provided to you where you lived.

Small shared houses might not always look very different from a small registered care home but a tenant has 'exclusive occupation', very different from a care home residency in an 'establishment'.

But other ideas were coming along. *Valuing People* (Department of Health, 2001) said that people could live in all kinds of settings and local authorities were encouraged to provide a wider range of housing options.

Now in 2009 there is a new report on services endorsing a cross government aim. A Public Service Agreement for people (PSA 16) will measure the progress in the numbers of adults with learning disabilities known to social services moving into settled accommodation (ie. not living in NHS campuses or residential care). This is a delivery priority for the government and local authorities. It means people having their own proper home.

What's the problem?

Whatever the drawbacks of older types of service, they were simple. You would be found a place providing accommodation and care, and if agreed, you go there. The local authority usually pays so the matter of choice is with them.

Now we want individual solutions, people able to choose their home and how they are supported – personalisation. Unlike the old system it's more complicated. Getting the right kind of housing is no easy matter. Do you own or rent, live on your own or with others? An individual budget is an aim and it is quite complicated to decide how it is made up. People need guidance and help with the practicalities.

What Housing Options sought to do was to treat people as customers and help them to plan and find what they want.

How does Housing Options work?

What Housing Options offers is good quality information and advice, which is hard to find elsewhere, on housing, funding, the law, and on planning for life.

Housing Options is funded in three ways:

- subscriptions from member organisations
- Department of Health grant and occasional charitable grants and donations
- fee income from workshops, publications and similar sources.

Housing Options provides mostly free services to families and people with learning disabilities through:

- telephone advice on housing, support, legal, benefits, and funding
- advice by letter or email
- a well used and regarded website
- a wide range of downloadable quick briefs and fact sheets.

Housing Options also depends on a membership that subsidises their free services and for whom they try to offer help so they can act as 'housing brokers' for those wanting

assistance. For more information about Housing Options go to their website (www. housingoptions.org.uk), email enquiries@housingoptions.org.uk or call 0845 465`496.

References

Brandon D (1989) How service brokerage works. *Community Living* **2** (4).

Department of Health (2001) *Valuing People: A new strategy for learning disability for the 21st century.* London: Department of Health.

Duffy S (2009) *Opening address*, The Big Event, 19 March, London.

Hatton C, Waters J, Duffy S, Senker J, Crosby N, Poll C, Tyson A, O'Brien J & Towell D (2008) *A Report on In Control's Second Phase: Evaluation and learning 2005–2007*, C Poll & S Duffy (Eds) London: In Control.

Rose SJ (1994) Canadian specific. *Community Care* **1010** 30–31.

Chapter 17

One family's experience

John Wallace

Introduction

This chapter is written from the perspective of a family with a disabled relative. It attempts to summarise the considerable benefits of personalisation but also to highlight a number of issues that need to be addressed if those benefits are to be fully realised. It concludes with more detailed discussions regarding resource allocation, accommodation and employment status. The last two topics have not received as much attention as resource allocation but they play an important part in helping disabled individuals attain a reasonable quality of life.

Family perspective on the benefits of personalisation

The author and his colleagues in Inclusion South West have developed personalised services in a variety of ways and have succeeded in creating significantly better quality of lives for the family members who are disabled. The major points to be drawn from this experience are as follows.

1. **Independent living** in a separate household is generally more satisfactory for the person than residential care, provided that adequate funding is available. This also applies to those who receive help within a family home.
2. **Control** over who is involved in helping the disabled individual is of crucial importance. The vast majority of people, including those with severe impairments, are able to exercise clear choices over who comes into their household. This applies not only to staff directly engaged but also provider staff and is fundamental to personalisation. (The right to choose should also apply to particular members of reviewing teams and prevent them entering a disabled person's home against their wishes).
3. **Direct contractual relationships** result in those who continue to use providers in their own homes being in a stronger position in terms of determining what and how help is provided. This flows naturally from the customer/supplier relationship between the user and the provider, just as it does for directly

engaged staff. Traditionally, the contractual relationship only involved the provider and local authority. Queries and complaints could readily be lost due to the triangular relationship and the individual's particular (personalised) needs not being reflected in the generic block contract. Similar benefits could also accrue to those in residential care through elimination of the local authority in the relationship.

4. **Flexibility and adaptability** become an integral part of the specification for the help provided. As a result, with commitment from all parties involved, successful solutions can be devised that are tailored specifically to the individual's difficulties, thus avoiding the unhelpful 'one size fits-all' approach.

Issues to be considered

In order to deliver the benefits of personalisation, there are a number of specific issues that need to be addressed. Some of the more important ones are set out below.

Long-term security and financial vulnerability

Families or individuals who choose to receive the direct payment form of individual budget are potentially vulnerable to arbitrary financial cuts. If a provider is offered insufficient funding, they can, ultimately, walk away from the problem and that strengthens their negotiating position. Families simply cannot and will not stop helping the individual family member live independently just because the budget has been exceeded or cut. This puts them at a considerable negotiating disadvantage. The individual budget contracts of the future must offer financial security such that if needs have not changed then the agreed budget must remain unchanged in RPI (retail prices index) inflation-adjusted terms. The individual budget must also be sufficient to cover associated costs for families or individuals organising their own help in the same way that adequate funding is given to providers of residential care.

The process of reviews and reassessments must be clearly defined and agreed as a part of the contract. Local authorities have a history of long-term contracts with providers and thus long-term security for individuals is equally achievable.

Outcomes focus

The move towards looking at outcomes rather than services is welcome as are moves to integrate/pool budget streams. However, there remains much confusion about what help individuals are entitled to receive. Resource allocation system (RAS) development could assist in overcoming this fundamental problem but, it must be emphasised, only if a systematic, evidence-based approach is adopted.

Management of individual budgets

The workload involved in organising and managing help can be considerable. At present, little help or guidance can be expected from local authorities. Relatives

involved in managing services will often find themselves working long hours for little or no financial reward in order to maximise the help provided to the disabled relative. No provider would accept such a situation and there is no reason why families should be treated any differently. Nor should the associated funding be the first to be cut on the basis that family carers can be expected to work unpaid on a permanent basis.

The key to eliminating this problem is to ensure that the management or co-ordination roles can, if desired, be bought in on a commercial basis and the decision as to which route is chosen is left to the individual or the family. In fact, this is already an often ignored requirement built in to the current Department of Health guidelines on direct payments calculation.

Contingency funding

Contingency funding is essential but the requirement for it can meet with resistance from local authorities. In real life, however good a support plan is, unpredictable events happen and circumstances change in ways that cannot be foreseen. The individual budget and direct payment contracts should allow for both increases in contingency funding and the return of unused funding. This is particularly important where the individual concerned has one or more fluctuating conditions. Having a pooled contingency fund across all users negates the benefits of personalisation.

Auditing

Financial auditing of direct payments has, in the past, caused a good deal of angst to families running more complicated services. However, the auditors have recently made a statement to the Association of Directors of Adult Social Services (ADASS) about a light touch regulation regime that recognises the new freedom inherent in individual budgets to spend money on the individual's priorities. Auditing requirements need to be discussed and agreed in any individual budget agreement. Local authorities need to evaluate the cost/benefit of auditing as a part of a more general efficiency review. What is the business case for continuing with the practice?

Regulated providers

Neither the individual nor the local authority should assume that engaging a provider to supply some or all the help needed will be trouble free or provide an adequate quality of service. Provider regulation largely seems to be a paper based policy and procedures exercise rather than an evaluation of the problems on the ground. For example, care agency staff are very variable in their quality; holiday and sickness cover is often non-existent and there is a constant tendency to invoice for more time than is actually provided (rounding upwards always). There are undoubtedly some good staff working for good providers but buying in help from providers is not a guarantee of quality. The support plan needs to make provision for negotiating with and managing provider-based services if that is the method of provision chosen.

Individual budgets should make providers accountable to those who are disabled. However, how well this works will depend on the relationship between the provider and the sponsoring local authority and the latter's relationship with the direct payment holder and their support circle. Some providers still cling to the belief that they are accountable only to the local authority. This is about a change in culture and delivery of service that has not actually yet taken root.

In-house local authority services

Most local authorities have some form of internal service provision. The following are important points.

1. The full costs, including departmental and corporate overheads are separately identified for providing these services.
2. The money for funding such services is included in the RAS and subsequent individual budget allocations. Individuals who want to use internal services can purchase them as an alternative to external provision. It is crucial that the user determines where the money is spent.

Only by adhering to these principles can one be sure that there is a fair and equitable division of resources. The ongoing demand for such internal services would become clear under these circumstances.

Legal assistance/insurance for employment issues

In an individual budget environment many disabled people or family members will engage staff to help them. There is a need to provide legal support to develop appropriate contracts and to provide some form of legal insurance to cover claims for all possible employment issues such as redundancy, unfair dismissal etc. The National Council on Independent Living (NCIL) has reported a number of such claims against disabled individuals who have no means of defending themselves. To be cost effective, the insurance cover needs to be negotiated at the local authority or at national level.

Legislation

There are a number of legislative issues that need to be rationalised as a part of the personalisation programme. At present, community care legislation and guidance is unchanged and some clarification of how it relates to personalisation would be welcome. The removal of ring-fencing of Supporting People funding and the new Right to Control funding streams other than social care (included in the current welfare reform bill) should lead to a more coherent allocation process. However, this will only happen if local authorities set out to achieve individual budgets that support multi-funding stream allocation of resources. This was the aim set out by *Improving the Life Chances of Disabled People* (Department of Health, 2005) and it is important that the message is not lost.

The Disability Equality Duty was introduced in December 2006 but is rarely, if ever, mentioned in the context of social care. It requires public bodies to involve (not just consult) with disabled individuals in the development of new policies and to produce impact assessments of proposed changes before they are implemented. It also requires public bodies to treat the disabled more favourably. All of these requirements should have a significant impact on the way in which personalisation is developed and implemented.

Efficiency improvements

The RAS, if correctly designed and implemented, should lead to an equitable slicing of the resources cake (using a CSCI analogy). However, the overall size of the cake is dependent on how efficient local authorities are. A largely 'missing' part of the personalisation programme should be concerned with improving internal efficiency and hence enlarging the cake. The auditor's recent ADASS statement about light touch auditing set the tone for local authorities to follow. At present, there appears to be no user-led or family-led scrutiny of this issue. This is a significant limitation of the existing arrangements that needs to be corrected urgently.

Pools of expertise/user-led organisations

Putting People First (Department of Health, 2007, p4) made the simple but important statement that families should be regarded as experts unless there is evidence to the contrary. It also laid emphasis on local user-led organisations being set up. It is worth making the following observations.

1. In addition to specific caring expertise, family members and disabled individuals themselves often have skills and experience in unrelated fields that could be productively employed in the personalisation programme. They represent an untapped pool of fresh thinking that is under-utilised at present.
2.   The general expectation should be that if that expertise is utilised, the individuals should be remunerated in a similar way to that in which local councillors are rewarded for public service.

Independent complaints procedure/judicial review

Everybody is aware that fundamental disagreements occur from time to time. In these circumstances, it is important that records of meetings are independently recorded and minuted. Facilities need to be made available and be seen to be independent of the parties involved. The requirement should be regarded as good practice, not as a confrontational request or act. At the simplest level, tape recordings (with two separate tapes) can be made of meetings so that the contents of minutes can be verified by both parties. There may, however, need to be independent witnesses or advocates present and some thought needs to be given as to how to provide such personnel when the situation demands it.

There is also the need for a more independent complaints procedure. A lack of real independence in current systems may be behind the rise in judicial review cases. The courts are less than enamoured with the current situation. Nor does judicial review deal with the substance of disagreements. It tends to concentrate only on procedural issues and matters of fact. Historically, this can leave broken relationships that still have to be managed. One of the principal aims of introducing the Disability Equality Duty was to avoid the need for individuals to take legal action. For whatever reason, there is a problem and new thinking is required to resolve matters in a less confrontational manner.

Resource allocation systems

In the physical world it is normal to measure quantities such as length, pressure, temperature and weight using instruments. Associated with such instrumentation are two familiar and well-accepted concepts.

1. A single instrument can only measure one quantity. For example, a tape measure is of little use when you want to measure weight or temperature.
2. Two instruments designed to measure a particular quantity can be different in their detailed construction but are expected to yield similar measurements in particular situations. For example, scales for weighing people can take many forms but a person weighing themselves on two scales of differing designs would expect to get similar readings because their weight is the same in both cases.

In fields such as education and social sciences, the instrument is a collection of questions because the quantities of interest cannot be directly measured. In education, the questions can be complex, but in the social sciences questionnaires with ordinal answers are normally employed. The quantities measured by such questionnaires are known as latent traits. In the context of a RAS, latent traits include general traits such as impact, variability, complexity and also more specific traits such self-care, safety, participation, economic well-being etc. Measurement scales for specific traits are often incorporated in the determination of general traits.

For the measurements to be valid and exhibit the fundamental characteristics outlined above, the questionnaire must conform to what is known as the Rasch model. The purpose of a RAS is to measure how much help people need and allocate resources accordingly. In principle, for the allocation to be valid it must be independent of the precise detail of questions being asked. If that allocation changes because specific questions are added or deleted, then the measurement and hence the allocation are invalid. It is also essential to know the level of uncertainty in the allocation. This explains the importance of designing a RAS that conforms to the Rasch model. Inclusion South West is hoping that a research programme based around the Rasch model will validate and/or improve the proposals now being developed by ADASS.

Financing of accommodation

Accommodation issues have not received as much attention as other parts of the personalisation agenda but they play a crucial role in shaping the well-being of the individual concerned. The following is designed to make people aware of some of the issues involved.

Needs

The location and type of accommodation required needs to be considered as a part of the support planning process. Without suitable accommodation, the rest of the plan will almost certainly fail. There are typically three scenarios to consider.

1. A move from residential care or long-term hospitalisation to a separate (independent) household or back to the family home.
2. A move from the family home to a separate (independent) household.
3. Staying in existing accommodation (eg. family home) but under changed circumstances and requiring modifications.

For benefit purposes, the term 'household' includes not only the obvious sources of accommodation (flats and houses) but also a unit of accommodation attached to a family home but with separate living accommodation. In such situations, a separate household can have shared bathroom and (possibly kitchen) facilities but must have separate living and bedroom accommodation with independent access. Detailed guidance is needed if this kind of arrangement is being considered.

Financing and housing benefit/local housing allowance

Financing of suitable accommodation can be a major obstacle to the implementation of the support plan. For many younger disabled adults looking to move into a separate household, the primary source of funding has been housing benefit (HB) (now local housing allowance, LHA), which allows the individual to rent accommodation. The following problems are most likely to occur.

1. LHA/HB payments are unrealistically low for the under 25s.
2. LHA/HB will only normally only pay for one bedroom accommodation for a single person renting in the private sector. This is a particular problem where the person requires 24/7 support from one or more persons who have to stay overnight.
3. Families are allowed to buy property and rent it to a family member but they are disbarred from doing so if the purpose of the arrangement is to defraud the local authority.
4. LHA/HB for supported housing arrangements may be limited to the standard rate (the so called Turnbull judgement).
5. For those whose accommodation needs exceed those available at standard LHA rates, higher rates are mainly only available to those renting from registered

social landlords or shared housing arrangements. By contrast, subsidised housing is common in care package arrangements with providers as it is just regarded as part of the overall cost.

Anybody can rent in the private sector and claim LHA (which is means tested). This arrangement is flexible but constraints on location exist because the LHA is fixed as an average over quite wide areas. Rents will vary across these areas and hence, in some cases, choice is restricted because the rents in the preferred locality are higher than LHA. In an individual budget (as opposed to direct payment) situation, it may be possible to use individual budget money to supplement LHA if the accommodation location issue is identified in the support planning process. Local authorities do have specific duties and powers in respect of accommodation (section 21 of the National Assistance Act (1948), Section 2 of the Local Government Act (2000)). If the additional accommodation needs are part of a person's assessed needs then additional payments should be included in the individual budget. However, the reality of what local authorities are prepared to do is unclear and needs clarifying. Security of tenure is always going to be an issue with the private rented sector.

If a family decides to buy and rent a property (as per item three) they may well be met with an initial blanket refusal to consider the arrangement by the frontline benefit staff. However, this potential refusal is misguided and legally ill-founded. There is well-established case law allowing this arrangement, provided that there is a proper tenancy agreement in place and the arrangement does not have fraudulent intent. Nor does the rent charged have to be a full commercial rent. Families considering this option need to be aware that the LHA is unlikely to cover the full cost of a mortgage and a substantial commitment of family savings capital (or surplus income to cover high mortgage payments) is likely to be required. Assistance with interest may be available in some circumstances from the benefit system but capital repayment remains a problem. The great benefits of the arrangement are that the family has complete control over the quality, location and suitability of the arrangement and the security of tenure is assured for the long term.

Families that part or fully own property should be aware that, in theory, landlords who also provide personal care should register with CSCI as the property could, in theory, be regarded as a care home. The consequential bureaucracy would be highly undesirable. Particularly in an individual budget situation, it is unlikely that CSCI would be interested in pursuing this technicality. Attitudes may depend on local relationships between individual budget/direct payment holders and the local authority, but it is an issue that needs to be clarified as a part of the personalisation agenda.

For many families or individuals, outright purchase of a suitable property is financially

impossible. Renting from a registered social landlord (RSL) may well be an option as RSLs are not constrained by LHA rates of rent and may provide higher quality accommodation. They are also able to provide suitable accommodation for those with particular higher than normal accommodation needs. However, RSL accommodation may not be available in a location that the family or the individual chose or the accommodation on offer may not be suitably adapted to the particular needs of the individual. In such situations, other more flexible supported housing or shared housing options may be available. The Turnbull judgement dealt a blow to the supported housing option for those with high accommodation needs. In such situations, the rent needs to be higher than HB/LHA standard rates but to qualify, the landlord is required to provide the care, support and supervision (and hence probably be registered with CSCI). This arrangement is contrary to good practice guidelines for ensuring secure tenancies. For example, if the provider of the care and support owns the property and pulls out of the contract, the person will get evicted and lose their home and neighbourhood support.

The government responded to Turnbull by introducing a new regulation in April 2008 that exempted shared ownership tenants (the tenancy is 'excluded') from the rental constraints. Thus shared ownership appears to be an ongoing option available to families. It has the advantages of being flexible in terms of location with good security of tenure. A possible downside of the arrangement is that it may be difficult to change who is providing help if the organisation who part own the property proves to be inadequate as a provider.

For those thinking about accommodation options, the Housing Options and MySafeHomes websites are useful starting places: (http://www.housingoptions.org.uk/) (http://www.mysafehome.info/).

Although targeted at those with learning difficulties they are of more general interest.

Employment status

Introduction

In many individual budget situations some or all of the money will be spent on engaging staff to provide help of one sort or another. One of the important questions that needs to be considered at the outset is that of employment status. The important question is of whether the person(s) being engaged is 'self-employed' or 'employed'?

The information provided below does not, of course, constitute proper legal advice but it should encourage individuals to investigate the matter further through appropriate channels. It should also be noted that employment status from a tax point of view is not necessarily the same as it is from either an employment tribunal or a health and safety

perspective. However, employment law and HM Revenue and Customs tax law line up fairly closely. Health and safety issues need to be considered quite separately.

Those involved in engaging staff should be aware that if an individual is paid on a 'self-employed' basis they are responsible for their own tax and national insurance contributions. However, if the 'self employed' person is really adjudged to have been 'employed', HM Revenue and Customs may challenge the person paying the employee and demand retrospective payment of outstanding tax and national insurance. This has happened and caused much distress to the disabled individuals concerned. Hence, it is important to be clear about employment status.

At first sight, 'self employment' status for carers/support workers seems unattractive from a disabled person's point of view. However, in practice, it has huge advantages in some circumstances. The process of engagement reduces to simply signing an appropriate contract and payment of invoices for work done. This is a major simplification for the disabled person or their representative compared with the attendant ongoing complexity of employing somebody.

Employment status overview

There are three simple facts that need to be recognised in considering the employment status of an individual. They are as follows.

1. The special tax commissioners are the final arbiters regarding employment status, not HM Revenue and Customs. Employment tribunals determine employment status when considering employment disputes.
2. A clear, comprehensive contract covering all the main issues must be in place. This contract must represent the reality of the arrangements, not a sham. For those who are employed, the contract will be a 'contract for service'. For those who are self-employed, the contract will be a 'contract for services'. Note the addition of subtle but important change of title.
3. The HM Revenue and Customs guidance on employment status is not complete. The general advice that personal assistants (PAs) funded by direct payments (or individual budgets in future) automatically have 'employment' status is not correct. Even the recent Department of Health guidance on direct payments concedes that self-employment is a possibility.

Factors that influence employment status

There are six factors that need to be looked at, the first three of which are the most important.

1. Personal services (and rights of substitution)

To be employed there must be a requirement for personal service. If the contract gives the individual an unfettered right of substitution then 'self-employment' status is appropriate. More usually, if the client has a right to veto substitution if the substitute does not have sufficient skills, 'self-employment' status is preserved. If the individual is actually substituted from time to time, then the case for 'self-employment' status is assured.

Anne Redston, senior tax partner at Ernst & Young pioneered the concept of self-employment in August 2003 when she assisted a mother with two severely disabled grown-up children to fight off an HM Revenue and Customs challenge. The carers, paid from a direct payment, self-organised a rota and all acted as substitutes for each other. The contracts clearly gave them the right of substitution and the special tax commissioners confirmed that these individuals were self-employed. As a result, HM Revenue and Customs was not able to demand backdated tax and national insurance from the mother. This was a lead case that HM Revenue and Customs chose not to mention but it established the principle that the right of substitution is an important factor in deciding on employment status. Be clear, however, that it did not set a precedent for all individual budget/ direct payments. Each case must be decided on its own merits.

2. Mutuality of obligation

For an 'employment' relationship to exist there must be an 'irreducible minimum of mutual obligation'. This obligation has to be more than simply being paid when the individual turns up. If the individual has the right to work when they want but are not obliged to on any particular day then it suggests a lack of mutuality and hence 'self-employment'. The contractual right to instant termination of the contract is also a pointer towards 'self-employment'.

In a care/support context, at first sight such arrangements may seem unattractive to the disabled person. However, in practice, cover arrangements usually have to be in place to cater for sickness, holidays and other emergencies. Hence, in reality, the fact that the carer/support worker can decide for themselves when they work is not, in practice, as bad as it seems. Furthermore, if the arrangement is unsatisfactory, instant termination of the contract is available without fear of recrimination or threats of unfair dismissal claims. This is a real problem for many disabled people who have little in the way of resources to defend themselves. It is also true that under such arrangements, the carer does not get paid for days they don't work and there are no payroll costs to be funded. Higher rates of pay can then be paid to the carer, thus helping to recruit higher quality staff and ensure a better service.

3. **Control**

   Many years ago, this used to be the sole determining factor in employment status, however, this is no longer the case. The term 'control' refers to the disabled person having a right to dictate to the caring individual what they do, when they do it, where they do it and how they do it. The first three are not as important as control over 'how'.

   Legally, what constitutes 'control' is not precisely defined. Some care/support workers act more in a supervisory/advisory role and the 'how' bit is very much down to them, thus further muddying the water. Given that personal service and mutuality of obligation can be much more clear-cut, it is probably not worth investing too much energy into clarifying this situation. As always, each situation has to be judged individually.

4. **Financial**

   Financial risk can be a useful indicator of employment status. Self-employed individuals inherently carry more financial risk. For example, invoices that may not be paid or paid late, instant termination without notice, lack of sick pay, liability for damage, and the costs associated with providing substitutes are all factors that make self-employment more financially risky. Payment by the hour and the use of timesheets are not indicators of 'employed' status. Self-employed carers are also obliged to correct defective work at their own expense (time) although this might be hard to enforce in some situations.

5. **In business on own account**

   In general, there are a number of minor factors to consider. However, the most relevant in the context of carers relates to the number of clients. An individual doing broadly similar work for several clients is almost certainly 'self-employed'. Local authorities setting up a register of PAs (a good idea in itself) should bear this in mind.

6. **Minor factors**

   There are a number of minor matters that need to be considered. For carers/support workers, the only one of significance is that working for the same client for years on end may be taken as a sign that the carer is an employee, not self-employed. However, this is not a strong argument and would probably only lead in itself to an 'employed' status if factors a, b and c all pointed towards 'employed' status.

A way forward

The intention of this section is to make the reader aware that employment status is not a straightforward issue. In the context of carers, both 'employed' and 'self-employed' status can be appropriate depending on the particular circumstances. From the

point of view of the disabled person, there are major simplification benefits to having 'self-employed' carer(s). However, in some cases, the (theoretical) security of having 'employed' carers who are obliged to turn up as agreed may be paramount. It is recommend that such issues are considered at the set up stage of a care package. Good legal advice needs to be made available such that whichever option the individual selects can be supported by properly constituted contractual documentation. This needs to be adequately funded in the direct payment or individual budget payments or generic legal advice provided by the local authority.

To minimise the overall cost and maximise clarity, perhaps local authorities (through ADASS) should jointly approach Anne Redston at Ernst and Young (the pioneer of self-employed PAs in the legal sense) with the intention of developing contractual templates that can be readily customised to individual circumstances. This is a specialist area and high quality legal advice is required to ensure disabled individuals are not put at financial risk.

In January 2008 the Chartered Institute of Taxation published a report entitled *Independent Living, Direct Payments and the Tax system*, which discusses various tax issues (including trust tax issues) for those with direct payments. It is a useful reference but does not give direct guidance on employment status and concedes that HM Revenue and Customs guidance is not always clear or helpful. Many of these tax issues could also benefit from an input from independent experts.

Acknowledgement

The above information regarding employment status is a very abbreviated summary of information provided by the Professional Contractors Group.

References

Chartered Institute of Taxation (2008) *Independent Living, Direct payments and the Tax System*. London: Chartered Institute of Taxation.

Department of Health (2005) *Improving the Life Chances of Disabled People*. London: Department of Health.

Department of Health (2007) *Putting People First: A shared vision and commitment to the transformation of adult social care*. London: Department of Health.